WORKBOOK

表达

描述 · 比较 · 介绍

DEVELOPING
CHINESE
FLUENCY

中级—高级中文教程
INTERMEDIATE – ADVANCED

张霓
PHYLLIS ZHANG

CENGAGE
Learning™

Andover • Melbourne • Mexico City • Stamford, CT • Toronto • Hong Kong • New Delhi • Seoul • Singapore • Tokyo

Developing Chinese Fluency
Phyllis Zhang

Publishing Director,
CLT Product Director:
Paul Tan

Editorial Manager:
Zhao Lan

Senior Graphic Designer:
Melvin Chong

Editor:
Titus Teo

Associate Development Editor:
Coco Koh

Product Manager (Outside Asia):
Mei Yun Loh

Senior Product Manager (Asia):
Joyce Tan

Assistant Publishing Manager:
Pauline Lim

Production Executive:
Cindy Chai

Country Manager (China):
Caroline Ma

Account Manager (China):
Arthur Sun

Photos:
Getty Images,
Photos.com

Illustrations:
Edwin Ng

Printed in Singapore
2 3 4 5 6 7 14 13 12 11

For product information and technology assistance, contact us at
Cengage Learning Asia Customer Support, 65-6410-1200

For permission to use material from this text or product, submit all requests online at **www.cengageasia.com/permissions**
Further permissions questions can be emailed to
asia.permissionrequest@cengage.com

ISBN-13: 978-981-4296-23-6

ISBN-10: 981-4296-23-6

Cengage Learning Asia Pte Ltd
5 Shenton Way #01-01
UIC Building
Singapore 068808

Cengage Learning is a leading provider of customized learning solutions with office locations around the globe, including Andover, Melbourne, Mexico City, Stamford (CT), Toronto, Hong Kong, New Delhi, Seoul, Singapore, and Tokyo. Locate your local office at: **www.cengage.com/global**

Cengage Learning products are represented in Canada by Nelson Education, Ltd.

For product information, visit our website at **www.cengageasia.com**

CENGAGE LEARNING

Asia Head Office (Singapore)

Cengage Learning Asia Pte Ltd
5 Shenton Way #01-01
UIC Building
Singapore 068808
Tel: (65) 6410 1200
Fax: (65) 6410 1208
Email: asia.info@cengage.com
Website: www.cengageasia.com

United States

Heinle Cengage Learning
20 Channel Center Street
Boston, MA 02210
USA
Tel: (1) 800 423 0563
Fax: (1) 800 487 8488
Email: higheredcs@cengage.com
Website: www.cengage.com/chinese

China

Cengage Learning Asia Pte Ltd
(Beijing Representative Office)
Room 1201, South Tower, Building C
Raycom Info Tech Park
No. 2, Kexueyuan South Road, Haidian District
Beijing, P.R.China 100190
Tel: (86) 10 8286 2096
Fax: (86) 10 8286 2089
Email: asia.infochina@cengage.com
Website: www.cengageasia.com

TO THE LEARNER

Is This the Right Course for You?

This course might **NOT** be suitable for you if your primary interests are one or more of the following:

- Learning basic language survival or coping skills.
- Improving listening and reading proficiency only.
- Reading literature or newspaper.

This course is probably **right** for you if you wish to build your speaking and writing proficiency within a relatively short time. It also offers solutions to these common experience and problems:

- Difficulty in making significant improvement in speaking skills, e.g., speech is too basic, often just lists of words, phrases, or broken and discrete sentences.
- Language barriers in daily communication and social occasions, e.g., feeling frustrated when trying to participate in a conversation of everyday topics with native speakers such as language partners or host parents.
- Inability to carry on a conversation with a native speaker in any breadth or depth.

Can This Course Replace an Advanced Reading Course?

This program includes a considerable amount of reading/listening passages to help build the learner's comprehension for upper intermediate to lower advanced levels. However, it is NOT designed for developing skills to read newspaper or literature. If you are already an <u>advanced speaker</u> and your goal is to develop proficiency in reading formal or literary style, then an <u>advanced reading course</u> might be more suitable for you.

What Would Be an Effective Learning Approach and Strategy for This Course?

Here are some recommendations for a successful and enjoyable learning experience:

1. *Be prepared for a skill training program:* Consider this course a systematic skill training program in which the initial stages usually involve mechanical drills that seem to discourage creativity. Keep in mind that these exercises are important steps to building your fluency and accuracy, and that you need to be patient and follow the training steps closely. The building of a strong foundation will facilitate more spontaneous and creative language use as you gain proficiency.

2. *Be clear about the training objectives:* In order to build your fluency up to the advanced level, this course is divided into several training units, each with clearly stated objectives. To better prepare yourself for the tasks in each unit, be sure to read the objectives.

3. *Learn vocabulary terms efficiently:* There is a considerable amount of vocabulary terms in each unit. While following the training procedures and self-testing guides in each unit, do develop your own strategies that work best for you. Follow the online study guide for better strategies that will help you learn the vocabulary more efficiently.

We hope that this program will help you build a strong foundation for advanced Chinese. Much of the success depends on your commitment and hard work. To get started, you may want to learn this famous saying from Laozi (老子), the ancient Chinese philosopher who is credited as the father of Taoism:

千里之行 始于足下
qiānlǐzhīxíng   shǐyúzúxià

"A journey of a thousand miles begins with a single step."

Phyllis Zhang

TABLE OF CONTENTS

第 一 单 元
UNIT 1
描述物体特征
DESCRIBING OBJECTS

第 一 课
Lesson 1

颜色与形状
COLORS AND SHAPES

 U1-1.2 词句操练 Aural-Oral Drills

There are **five** drills in this lesson, which can be completed in one session (*30 min.*). You need to complete each section twice to achieve intended results.

Important note: Before starting each drill, be sure to preview the glossary for an initial familiarization with the new words and expressions to be covered (*follow the glossary number as indicated in each drill*). For best results, also type the new words between or after the two rounds.

U1-1.2-A 说颜色 [词汇 U1.2]

看图跟读
Listen to and read each word aloud. Memorize the words.

1. 红色、黄色、蓝色、绿色、棕色、紫色、黑色、灰色、米色、白色、透明/无色

2. 深色、浅色、深红色、浅蓝色、天蓝色、粉红色、深棕色、浅灰色

For the following items, pay special attention to the use of a color word + a noun.

3. (*Monosyllabic color word + Noun*: "的" is not used)

    红包、黑板、黄花、蓝笔

4. (*Polysyllabic color words + Noun*)

    粉红色的笔、大红色的书包、彩色(的)屏幕、黑白(的)电视

U1-1.2-B 颜色和物品 [词汇 U1.0; 1.2]

看图跟读，并回答问题
While looking at the picture(s), repeat each word you hear and try to memorize it. Then answer the questions.

1. **看图跟读:** 窗帘、灯、地毯、桌子、桌布、花瓶、沙发、墙、画、电视机柜
   回答问题: 这里有些什么？是什么颜色的？哪些是深色/浅色的？

2. **看图跟读:** 书桌、台灯、杯子、纸、笔、剪刀、文件夹、公文包
   回答问题: 这里有些什么？每个东西是什么颜色的？

3. **看图跟读:** 书架、床、床单、衣柜、书包、椅子
   回答问题: 这里有些什么？每个东西是什么颜色的？

U1-1.2-C 对颜色的喜好 [词汇 U1.0; 1.2]

回答问题
Answer the following questions on **personal preferences**.

1. 这里有不同颜色的书包。你喜欢哪个颜色的?
2. 你的书包是什么颜色的？你的桌子呢?
3. 你喜欢用哪一种文件夹，透明的还是不透明的?
4. 用彩色的纸写通知 (announcement), 你喜欢用深色的还是浅色的?

U1-1.2-D 形状、图案 [词汇 U1.3-1.4]

看图跟读，然后回答问题

While looking at the picture(s), repeat each word you hear and try to memorize it. Then answer the questions.

1. **看图跟读:** 正方形、长方形、三角形、圆形、椭圆形、菱形、圆柱形、圆锥形、桃/心形、五角形、多边形

2. **看图跟读:** 直线条、斜线条、弯线、横线、竖线、波浪纹、锯齿纹、格子纹、网纹

3. **回答问题:** 这张画上有什么形状、线条，或花纹？

4. **回答问题:** 这是一张什么形状的桌子：长方形、正方形，还是圆形？

5. **回答问题:** 桌上放着一个什么形状的笔筒：圆锥形还是圆柱形？

6. **看图回答问题:**

　　1) 这张餐桌是什么形状的: 长方形、正方形、圆形？

　　2) 桌布是什么色的: 浅色还是深色？

　　3) 桌布上有什么花纹图案：格子纹、波浪纹、网纹？

U1-1.2-E 谈谈你身边的东西

Part 1: Answer the questions as quickly as possible. You have only a few seconds for each question.

1. 你最喜欢的颜色是什么？

2. 你的床单是什么颜色？

3. 你现在穿的衣服上面有花纹图案吗？

4. 你房间里什么颜色比较多？

5. 你房间里有没有菱形和椭圆形的东西？

6. 你桌子上有没有圆柱形的东西？

7. 如果你有一间自己的房间，你希望墙是什么颜色的？

8. 你认为颜色和人的喜好有没有关系？ (xǐhào / likes, preferences)

Part 2: Answer the following questions as quickly as possible. You have only a few seconds for each question.

你同意不同意下面的说法？

1. 喜欢红色的人比较热情。(rèqíng / passionate, warm-hearted)

2. 喜欢红色的人多半是急性子。(jíxìngzi / impetuous)

3. 喜欢白色的人比较爱干净。(gānjìng / clean)

4. 喜欢蓝色的人最喜欢运动和旅游。(lǚyóu / travel)

5. 喜欢粉红色的人很浪漫。(làngmàn / romantic)

流利强化 Fluency Enhancement

U1-1.7 语块练习：颜色、形状、图案 [词汇 U1.0-1.4]

Chunking Exercise: First read each phrase out loud, and then type the phrase. For output efficiency and accuracy, type in words or chunks (e.g., for "红色的书包", enter "*hongsede shubao*" or "*hongsedeshubao*" instead of each syllable or character individually). Be sure to check your Chinese characters for accuracy after each phrase is entered.

1. 红色的书包， 深蓝色的本子， 透明的文件夹， 金黄色的笔， 彩色的纸， 黑色的剪刀
   hóngsède shūbāo shēnlánsède běnzi tòumíngde wénjiànjiā jīnhuángsède bǐ cǎisède zhǐ hēisède jiǎndāo

2. 米色的沙发， 浅色的窗帘， 咖啡色的桌子， 深红色的地毯， 紫色的花瓶
   mǐsède shāfā qiǎnsède chuānglián kāfēisède zhuōzi shēnhóngsède dìtǎn zǐsède huāpíng

3. 圆桌， 圆形的房子， 长方形的桌子， 椭圆形的屋子， 多边形的笔筒
   yuánzhuō yuánxíngde fángzi chángfāngxíngde zhuōzi tuǒyuánxíngde wūzi duōbiānxíngde bǐtǒng

4. 线条图案， 波浪线的花纹/波浪纹， 格子花纹的桌布， 带竖线条的衣服
   xiàntiáo tú'àn bōlàngxiànde huāwén bōlàngwén gézihuāwénde zhuōbù dàishùxiàntiáode yīfu

5. 黑白图片， 彩色屏幕(彩屏)， 透明的三角形台灯， 深色的电视机柜
   hēibái túpiàn cǎisèpíngmù cǎipíng tòumíngde sānjiǎoxíng táidēng shēnsède diànshìjīguì

U1-1.8 流利练习：描述颜色、形状

Fluency Drill: Listen to or read the following items sentence by sentence. You should repeat each sentence until you can say the sentence smoothly and accurately with the correct tones. Then for each item, say the sentences from memory. Long sentences are separated by lines for appropriate grouping.

1. 桌子上|有一个深蓝色的本子|和一个透明的文件夹，还有一个黑色的笔筒。笔筒里面有一些彩色的笔|和一把红色的剪刀。

2. 客厅的墙是浅棕色的，窗帘是咖啡色的。客厅里|有一张大红色的沙发、一个黑色的茶几，还有一块|深红色的地毯。

3. 这张餐桌看上去很不错，是长方形的，上面是一块米色的桌布，桌布上|有一些很漂亮的浅色的花纹图案；桌子上|还有一个浅色的花瓶|和一些黄色的花。

U1-1.9 速读/巩固：《中国人怎么看颜色？》（5 分钟）

Speed Reading/Review: Follow the steps below.

1. Read the passage "中国人怎么看颜色？" in Lesson 1 within three minutes, focusing on meaning.
2. Without looking at the book, recall the details.
3. Read the entire passage one more time, focusing on expressions.

第 二 课 | **外形特点**
Lesson 2 | FORMS OF OBJECTS

 U1-2.2 词句操练 Aural-Oral Drills

There are <u>nine</u> drills in this lesson, which can be completed in two sessions (*A to F for 30 min., and G to I for 20 min.*). You need to complete each drill twice to achieve intended results.

Important note: Before starting each drill, be sure to preview the glossary for an initial familiarization with the new words and expressions to be covered (*follow the glossary number as indicated in each drill*). For best results, also type the new words between or after the two rounds.

U1-2.2-A 描述外形特征 [词汇 U1.6]

看图跟读，然后回答问题

Look at the picture(s) and repeat the sentence you hear. Then answer the question based on the information.

看图跟读	回答问题
1. 这个东西是<u>片状</u>的。	→ 这个东西的外形有什么特征？ （回答：这个东西是片状的。）
2. 这个东西是<u>管状</u>的。	→ 这个东西有什么特征？
3. 这个东西是<u>块状</u>的。	→ 那个东西是片状的吗？
4. 这个东西是<u>网状</u>的。	→ 那个东西是板状的还是块状的？

U1-2.2-B 表达形体 [词汇 U1.7]

看图跟读，然后回答问题

For each item, look at the picture and repeat the sentence you hear. Then answer the question based on this initial information.

看图跟读	回答问题
1. 电话线很长，绳子很短。	→ 电话线和绳子都很长吗？
2. 书桌比较宽，书架有点窄。	→ 书桌和书架是宽还是窄？
3. 这本书很厚，那本比较薄。	→ 这两本书都很厚吗？
4. 这根绳子/管子有点细，不够粗。	→ 这根绳子/管子粗不粗？
5. 这把尺子太短了，不够长。	→ 这把尺子很长吗？
6. 这枝铅笔有点秃，不够尖。	→ 这枝铅笔尖不尖？
7. 这个瓶子是扁的。	→ 这个瓶子是什么形状的？
8. 这个瓶子是空的，那个是满的。	→ 这两个瓶子都是空的吗？

U1-2.2-C 用反义词 [词汇 U1.7]

This drill works on some common *antonym* pairs to describe the forms of objects. Review the three forms below:

> **Antonyms:** 宽 — 窄　高 — 矮　长 — 短　粗 — 细
> 　　　　　　kuān　zhǎi　gāo　ǎi　cháng　duǎn　cū　xì

These three forms with antonym pairs conveys the idea of difference in size, height etc.

1. 有A有B：这些桌子有大有小。(These tables come in different sizes.)

2. AABB：　这些桌子大大小小。(These tables are different in size.)

3. AB不一：这些桌子大小不一。(These tables vary in size.)

跟读, 然后回答问题

First repeat the sentence you hear. Then answer the question, applying one of the three forms.

看图跟读	回答问题
1. 这些桌子有宽有窄。	→ 那些桌子宽还是窄?
	(回答：那些桌子有宽有窄/宽宽窄窄 / 宽窄不一。)
2. 这几个书架高高矮矮。	→ 那些书架都很高吗?
3. 这些线粗粗细细。	→ 那些线都一样细吗?
4. 这些管子/棍子粗细不一。	→ 那些管子/棍子都是粗的吗?

U1-2.2-D 用复合形容词 [词汇 U1.7]

This drill works on some *compound adjectives* used to describe the forms of objects.

> **Compound adjectives:** 细长　　宽大　　矮小　　高大
> 　　　　　　　　　　　xìcháng　kuāndà　ǎixiǎo　gāodà

These compound adjectives are commonly used as one word (A+B), or expanded into four-character phrases (又A又B or AABB). Unlike an antonym pair, however, these four-character phrases add an emphatic tone with the adverb form "both... and..." (又A又B), or vividness with the reduplication form (AABB).

> 高大 (tall and big)　→　又高又大 (both tall and big)　　高高大大 (tall and big)

跟读原句，然后改换为四字短语

First repeat the sentence you hear, and then rephrase the sentence using one of the four-character forms.

跟读	改换词语
1. 这里有几根细长的管子。	→ 这里有几根又细又长/细细长长的管子。
2. 这是一个宽大的房间。	→
3. 这是一个矮小的柜子。	→
4. 我想买一个高大的书架。	→

U1-2.2-E "变"字的用法

看图回答问题

Look at the pictures and answer the following questions.

1. 这个东西现在是什么形状?
2. 形状变了没有?
3. 变大了还是变小了?
4. 现在变粗了还是变细了?
5. 现在有什么变化? 变得更粗了还是更细了?
6. 最后变成什么了?

U1-2.2-F 反义词 [词汇 U1.7]

> ***Antonyms:*** 长 — 短 宽 — 窄 粗 — 细 厚 — 薄

1. 这本书太＿＿＿＿＿＿＿，三天看不完，我还是借那本＿＿＿＿＿＿＿的吧。

2. 这根线太＿＿＿＿＿＿＿了，不够＿＿＿＿＿＿＿，换一根吧。

3. 这种管子太＿＿＿＿＿＿＿了，那种管子比较＿＿＿＿＿＿＿。

4. 因为书架上的板子不够＿＿＿＿＿＿＿，所以板子都弯了，不平了。

5. 这张床太宽了，房间非常＿＿＿＿＿＿＿，可能放不下。

U1-2.2-G 描述状态：Position V着 [词汇 U1.8]

This drill works on the "V着" structure with positional verbs to describe the state of an object or a scene (see notes in the Textbook). Review these verbs first:

> 放　堆　铺　挂　贴　停　种　画　写
> fàng　duī　pū　guà　tiē　tíng　zhòng　huà　xiě

转换句式:　Position 有……　➔　Position V着……

For each item, first look at the picture and repeat the sentence you hear. Then rephrase the sentence using the verb form provided.

例：桌子上<u>有</u>一个电视机。　（放着）　➔　桌子上<u>放着</u>一个电视机。

1. 床上有很多衣服。　　　　（放着/堆着）➔
2. 床上有一块白色的床单。（铺着）　➔
3. 桌子上有一块格子的桌布。（铺着）➔
4. 墙上有几张相片。　　　（贴着）　➔
5. 墙上有一张国画。　　　（挂着）　➔
6. 纸上有不同的形状和线条。（画着）➔
7. 墙上有很多字。　　　　（写着）　➔
8. 这里有很多自行车。　　（停着）　➔
9. 门外面有一些漂亮的花。（种着）　➔

U1-2.2-H 描述状态：Position V满了 [词汇 U1.8]

转换句式

This drill works on two patterns, "**Position V着**" and "**Position V满了**", with the latter expressing "full of". Repeat the sentence you hear. Then restate the sentence by using the "V满了" form.

> Position V着……　➔　Position V满了……

例：桌子上<u>放着</u>很多书。　　　　➔　　　　桌子上<u>放满了</u>书。

1. <u>床上</u><u>堆着</u>很多衣服。 →

2. 墙上<u>贴着</u>很多图片。 →

3. 门外面<u>停着</u>很多车。 →

4. 门外面<u>种着</u>很多花。 →

5. 纸上<u>画着</u>很多线条。 →

6. <u>纸上</u><u>写着</u>很多字。 →

U1-2.2-I 回答问题：谈谈自己身边的物品 [词汇 U1.8]

Answer the following questions to master the question and negation forms for "V着" and "V满了". In the second round, repeat each question before answering it.

Use "没" for <u>negation</u> of "V着" and "V满了" to answer the question form "<u>是不是</u> V着……?", or "<u>有没有</u>……?"

例：

<u>纸上没写着字</u>；桌子上没放满书。　(Do not include "了" in the negative sentence.)

纸上是不是/有没有写着很多字?　→　对, 纸上写着很多字。
　　　　　　　　　　　　　　　　　　不是/没有, 纸上没写着很多字。

1. 你的桌子上**放着**一个台灯吗?

2. 你的书架上是不是**放满了**书?

3. 你的书桌上是不是**堆着**很多东西?

4. 你房间的墙上有没有**贴着**或者**挂着**什么?

5. 你的床上是不是**堆着**很多东西?

6. 你房间的地上有没有**铺着**地毯?

7. 你的中文书上**写着**什么?

8. 你的房间里是不是**挂着**窗帘?

9. 你的房子外面**种着**树和花吗?

10. 你的房子外面**停着**车吗?

流利强化 Fluency Enhancement

U1-2.7 语块练习

Chunking Exercise: First read each phrase aloud, and then type it out. For output efficiency and accuracy, type in words or chunks instead of each character individually (e.g., for "很长的管子", type "henchangde guanzi" or "henchangdeguanzi").
Note that your computer might not distinguish between "有A有B" and "又A又B" phrases correctly, so you might need to type these phrases character by character. Check your character accuracy, especially for "又", "有", and "矮" in this exercise.

U1-2.7-A 描述物体形状 [词汇 U1.5-1.7]

Using *Antonyms*

管子：很长的管子，很短的管子，长长短短的管子，这些管子有长有短

杆子：很粗的杆子，很细的杆子，粗粗细细的杆子，这些杆子有粗有细，粗细不一

架子：很高的架子，很矮的架子，高高矮矮的架子，这些架子有高有矮，高矮不一

板子：很厚的板子，很薄的板子，厚厚薄薄的板子，这些板子有厚有薄，厚薄不一

Using *compound adjectives*

棍子：细长的棍子，很细很长的棍子，又细又长的棍子，细细长长的棍子

架子：高大的架子，很高很大的架子，又高又大的架子，高高大大的架子

屋子：很宽大的屋子，很宽很大的屋子，又宽又大的屋子，宽宽大大的屋子

柜子：很矮小的柜子，很矮很小的柜子，又矮又小的柜子，矮矮小小的柜子

U1-2.7-B 描述状态 (V着/V满了)［词汇 U1.8］

Long sentences are separated by lines for appropriate grouping.

1. 很多黄色的花：他家的门口 |种着很多 |黄色的花。

2. 花花绿绿的衣服：那张床上 |堆满了 |花花绿绿的衣服。

3. 大大小小的图片，五颜六色的图片：墙上贴着 |大大小小 |五颜六色的图片。

4. 几辆自行车、一些报纸：外面停着 |几辆自行车，旁边堆着 |一些报纸。

5. 彩色线条和图案：纸上画着 |很多彩色线条和图案。

6. 各种颜色的字：纸上写满了 |各种颜色的字。

7. 长长短短的管子：房子里放着 |很多长长短短的管子。

8. 厚厚薄薄的书：架子上放着 |一些厚厚薄薄的书。

9. 一块鲜红色的地毯：地上铺着 |一块鲜红色的地毯。

10. 一块雪白的桌布，一瓶红色的鲜花：桌上铺着 |一块雪白的桌布，上面放着 |一瓶红色的鲜花。

U1-2.8 流利练习：描述物体外形［词汇 U1.8］

Fluency Drill: Listen to the whole sentence, pause for <u>two</u> to <u>three</u> seconds, and then say it aloud <u>from memory</u>. You should repeat an item until you can say it smoothly and accurately.

> 改成　换成　漆成　变大　做高　画大

1. 我喜欢矮柜子，所以我想把这个高柜子<u>改成矮的</u>。

2. 我想把这张圆桌<u>换成</u>一张方桌，你看怎么样？

3. 这些线条太粗了，是不是可以<u>画细一点</u>？

4. 这张桌子<u>矮了一点</u>，我们可以把它<u>做高一点</u>。

5. 我不喜欢<u>白色的书架</u>，所以我想把这个书架<u>换成黑色的</u>。

6. 这个房间以前是<u>紫色的</u>，后来我把它<u>漆成浅绿色</u>的了。

7. 我觉得这个长方形<u>有点小</u>，可不可以把它<u>变大一点</u>？

8. 这张纸的颜色太深了，能不能<u>改成浅色的</u>？

第一单元 · 描述物体特征

U1-2.9 写作练习：现在是什么样？想变成什么样？ （10分钟）

Writing Exercise: Imagine you are unhappy with your apartment and want to make some alterations. You write to a contractor to describe what your rooms are like now, and what changes you want to make. Use the following expressions and verb forms.

> 太……了　　不够……　　又A又B　　想把＿＿＿变成……
>
> 变得……　　换成……　　漆成……　　变宽/窄

U1-2.10 词语自测：颜色与形状；外形特点 （5分钟)

Vocabulary Self-Testing: Test yourself on the words and expressions in at least three of the following categories:

1. Colors, shapes, lines and patterns

2. Forms of objects (opposites: wide/narrow, etc.)

3. Living-room items

4. Bedroom items

5. Office items

Suggestions:

1. **English-to-Chinese**: Use the English glossary of each section, covering the Chinese characters. Say each item aloud in Chinese as you read it in English. Mark the ones you fail to reproduce in Chinese for review (*you may also use flashcards*).

2. **Chinese-to-English**: Reverse the above to work on comprehension and character recognition. Mark the difficult characters for extra review.

3. **Memory Test**: Time yourself for three minutes and try to reproduce as many vocabulary items in the categories listed above as possible. You can type the items out in pinyin so that you don't lose count. When your time is up, go over the same sections in the vocabulary glossary to see what you have missed. Then test yourself again to improve your performance.

第 三 课 | **描述视觉印象**
Lesson 3 | DESCRIBING VISUAL
IMPRESSIONS

 U1-3.2 词句操练 Aural-Oral Drills

There are <u>four</u> drills in this lesson, which can be completed in one session (*30 min.*). You need to complete each drill twice to achieve intended results.

Important note: Before starting each drill, be sure to preview the glossary for an initial familiarization with the new words and expressions to be covered (*follow the glossary number as indicated in each drill*). For best results, also type the new words between or after the two rounds.

U1-3.2-A 形容颜色和图像 [词汇 U1.9-1.10]

看图回答问题

Listen to each question and then answer it with the appropriate word. In the second round, repeat each question before answering it.

回答问题	提示
1. 中国的国旗有什么特点？	很鲜艳、不够明快、很暗淡
2. 中国钱的颜色有什么特点？	单调、丰富、鲜艳、沉闷、暗淡
3. 中国古代的房子的颜色怎么样？	比较单调、很丰富、有点沉闷
4. 这张画是什么色调？	暖色调、冷色调、柔和的色调
5. 这张画的色彩怎么样？	比较浓、比较淡、很浅、很深
6. 这张画的颜色有什么特点？	很柔和、很鲜艳、很单调、很沉闷
7. 这张画的线条和花纹怎么样？	很清晰、有点模糊、不够细腻
8. 这张照片看上去怎么样？	很清晰、有点模糊、不够细腻
9. 这个电视机的图像怎么样？	很清晰、不够清晰、有点模糊
10.这个手机的图像怎么样？	很清晰、不够清晰、有点模糊

U1-3.2-B 形容颜色和图案/图像 [词汇 U1.9-1.10]

Read the sentence aloud, and then rephrase it using the "**不够……**" form with an opposite meaning as shown in the example.

> 换一种说法: "不够……"

例：这张画的颜色有点暗淡。 → 这张画的颜色不够鲜艳、明快。

1. 这张照片颜色有点浅。 → （深）

2. 那个房间的颜色比较单调。 → （丰富）

3. 这个窗帘的颜色有点沉闷。 → （明快）

4. 这张照片有点儿模糊。 → （清晰）

第一单元 · 描述物体特征

U1-3.2-C 回答问题: 谈谈自己的物品 [词汇 U1.9-1.11]

Answer the questions as if you were chatting with a Chinese friend. In the second round, repeat each question before answering it.

回答问题	提示
1. 现在你房间里的颜色怎么样？	单调沉闷、非常丰富、很柔和、很协调
2. 你希望自己房间的墙是什么色调的？	暖色调、冷色调、白色
3. 你的房间还有什么特点？	非常明亮、比较黑/比较暗、有点沉闷
4. 你喜欢什么样的床单？	鲜艳明快、色彩柔和、色彩深沉
5. 你喜欢什么色调的衣服？	鲜艳明快、五颜六色、柔和协调
6. 你喜欢什么样的书包？	鲜艳明快、色彩深沉、色彩丰富
7. 哪一种色调的窗帘比较适合你的喜好？	柔和、明快、鲜艳、深沉
8. 如果在房间里挂一张画，你要什么色调的？	浓色调、淡色调、黑白的、五颜六色的

U1-3.2-D 比喻用法 [词汇 U1.12]

This drill works on using analogies to describe color. The two patterns introduced here are similar in meaning.

Pattern 1		Pattern 2
像……一样(红)	→	(红)得像……一样/似的
... is (red) like...		... is so (red) that it resembles...

转换句式

First, repeat the sentence in Pattern 1, and then rephrase it using Pattern 2, as shown in the example.

例：她的衣服(的颜色)像火一样红 。   →   她的衣服红得像火一样/似的。

1. 她的衣服像血一样红。 →

2. 这个墙的颜色像天一样蓝。 →

3. 这个墙的颜色像海一样蓝。 →

4. 杯子里的水像牛奶一样白。 →

5. 她的脸像雪一样白。 →

6. 她的脸像纸一样白 (pale)。 →

7. 这个窗帘的颜色像草一样绿。 →

8. 这个颜色像金子一样黄。 →

流利强化 Fluency Enhancement

 U1-3.9 语块练习：形容颜色、花纹、图案 [词汇 U1.9-1.11]

Chunking Exercise: First read each of the following phrases aloud, and then type it out. **Note:** for "图案", type "tu'an". Be sure to check your Chinese characters for accuracy after each phrase is entered.

1.	鲜艳的颜色， xiānyànde yánsè	鲜艳的色调， xiānyànde sèdiào	色调很鲜艳， sèdiào hěnxiānyàn	色调鲜艳的图案， sèdiàoxiānyànde tú'àn	颜色鲜艳的图画 yánsèxiānyànde túhuà
2.	深沉的颜色， shēnchénde yánsè	暗淡的颜色， àndànde yánsè	色调比较深沉， sèdiào bǐjiàoshēnchén	色调有点暗淡， sèdiào yǒudiǎnàndàn	颜色暗淡的图案 yánsèàndànde tú'àn
3.	柔和的颜色， róuhéde yánsè	协调的颜色， xiétiáode yánsè	色调比较柔和， sèdiào bǐjiàoróuhé	颜色不太协调， yánsè bútàixiétiáo	房间的色调很柔和 fángjiānde sèdiào hěnróuhé
4.	颜色很浓， yánsè hěnnóng	颜色很淡， yánsè hěndàn	颜色不浓不淡， yánsè bùnóngbúdàn	这个颜色比那个浓 zhègèyánsè bǐ nàgè nóng	
5.	色彩很丰富， sècǎi hěnfēngfù	有点单调， yǒudiǎn dāndiào	色彩丰富的图案， sècǎifēngfùde tú'àn	色彩不够丰富， sècǎi búgòufēngfù	色彩单调的图画 sècǎidāndiàode túhuà
6.	鲜艳明快的颜色， xiānyànmíngkuàide yánsè	花花绿绿的衣服， huāhuālùlùde yīfu	单调沉闷的颜色， dāndiàochénmènde yánsè	五颜六色的图案 wǔyánliùsède tú'àn	
7.	清晰的线条， qīngxīde xiàntiáo	细腻的花纹， xìnìde huāwén	模糊的线条花纹， móhude xiàntiáohuāwén	花纹不够清晰， huāwén búgòuqīngxī	图案有点模糊 tú'àn yǒudiǎnmóhu

U1-3.10 语句练习：动词句式、形容词语 [词汇 U1.9-1.12]

Listen to or read each sentence. Pause for <u>three</u> seconds, say the whole sentence aloud <u>from memory</u>, and then type the sentence out. Retype the sentence until you get 100% accuracy. Type in whole phrases or chunks. Long sentences are separated by lines for appropriate grouping.

1. 这边的墙上|都贴满东西了，我看就把这张画|挂在那面墙上吧。
2. 别把书|都堆在床下面，你可以把那些薄的|放在我的书架上。
3. 这个房间的颜色|太单调了，我们在茶几这里|铺一块颜色鲜艳的地毯吧。
4. 这个桌布|颜色太深了，和这个房间|不太协调，换一块柔和一点的吧。
5. 这个教室里|色彩很丰富，到处贴着五颜六色的图片|和孩子们画的图画。
6. 她觉得深沉的颜色|有点沉闷，她喜欢|色彩丰富、鲜艳明快的颜色。
7. 这张画是绿色调的，草和叶子的颜色|绿得就像真的似的。
8. 这张画太旧了，上面的花纹图案|已经不够清晰了，有的线条很模糊，颜色也不够鲜艳明快了。
9. 这种红色非常鲜艳，红得像火一样，会让人感到兴奋。
10. 我想把暖色调|改成冷色调，这样会给人一种|安静的感觉。

第一单元 · 描述物体特征

U1-3.11 流利练习

U1-3.11-A 比较颜色和色调

Fluency Drill: Listen to the following comparison sentences. After each sentence, pause for _two_ to _three_ seconds, and then repeat the whole sentence aloud _from memory_. You should repeat each sentence until you can say the sentence smoothly and accurately with the correct tones. Long sentences are separated by lines for appropriate grouping.

1. 从色调上看，这张画和那张画很不一样。

2. 在颜色方面，这张画是冷色调，不如那张鲜艳。

3. 那张画的色彩比这张的更丰富，看上去五颜六色、花花绿绿的。

4. 从色调上看，这张画有点单调沉闷，多半是灰色和黑色。

5. 这张画的线条|不如那张清晰，有点模糊。

6. 这个图案的颜色|比那个的柔和多了，没有很浓的|大红大绿的颜色。

7. 这个图上的花纹|看上去比那个图的细腻，而且|色彩也更丰富一点。

8. 这个房间的颜色|没有那个房间的丰富，但比那个房间的协调多了。

U1-3.11-B 《挂几张画怎么样？》 (5分钟)

Fluency Drill: First listen to the dialogue "挂几张画怎么样" once for comprehension. Then play the audio clip sentence by sentence. After each sentence, pause for _two_ seconds, and then say the whole sentence aloud mimicking the tone of speech. You should repeat each sentence until you can say it out smoothly and accurately with emotion.

 U1-3.12 速读/巩固：《国画》 (5分钟)

1. Read the passages about "国画" in Lesson 3 within _three_ minutes, focusing on words and expressions.

2. Without looking at the book, recall the details in Chinese.

3. Read the passages again and learn the new words and useful expressions.

U1-3.13 写作练习：比较绘画特点 (10分钟)

Writing Exercise: Describe the main features of traditional paintings in your culture, such as use of color and lines. Discuss briefly how they are similar to or different from the traditional Chinese paintings in general terms without getting into technical details. See the comparative expressions in the Appendices of the Textbook.

U1-3.14 词语自测：描述视觉印象 (5 分钟)

Vocabulary Self-Testing: Test yourself on these items:

1. _Descriptive adjectives_ and four-character phrases for color, tone, lines and patterns (e.g., _bright, dull_...)
2. _Positional verbs_ and their _noun_ partners with appropriate measures (e.g., 铺着一块桌布)

Suggestions:

1. **English-to-Chinese:** Use the English glossary of each section, covering the Chinese characters. Say each item aloud in Chinese as you read it in English. Mark the ones you fail to reproduce in Chinese for review (_you may also use flashcards_).

2. **Chinese-to-English:** Reverse the above to work on comprehension and character recognition. Mark the difficult characters for extra review.

3. **Memory Test:** Time yourself for _two_ minutes and try to reproduce as many vocabulary items in the categories listed above as possible. You can type the items out in pinyin so that you don't lose count. When your time is up, go over the same sections in the vocabulary glossary to see what you have missed. Then test yourself again to improve your performance.

第 四 课　**描述场景与空间**
Lesson 4　DESCRIBING A SCENE
OR SPACE

U1-4.1 & 4.2 描述静态空间和空间布置

Read the sample paragraphs in this lesson, paying special attention to **sentence connections** and **transitions**. Also note the use of **punctuation marks** (*e.g., commas are used between sentences within a subtopic*). Then read it (*or play the audio clip*) sentence by sentence. Try to memorize the whole or part of the paragraph(s) to improve your feel of the structure and language use.

单元测试与报告 Unit Assignments

For the unit review and assignments, please consult Appendices 1-3 for a guide on language use, grammar, and discourse structure.

U1-4.3 词语测试：本单元词语句式及语言结构

Vocabulary Test: Review the words and expressions in this unit and be prepared for a written test on vocabulary, word usage, and sentence forms, among others.

U1-4.4 口头报告：描述空间、画面

Oral Assignment: Be prepared to complete the following simulation tasks. You must describe everything clearly without using visual aids. The preparation can be done in small groups. Your teacher may choose one of these scenarios:

- 你到中国的一个小学做老师，看到他们的教室单调沉闷，除了桌椅和黑板以外什么都没有。你想重新布置、装饰一下，所以向学校的老师描述你的想法，并说明为什么想做这样的改变。

  You are teaching in an elementary school in China and find that their classrooms look plain. There are only desks, chairs, and blackboards. You have a plan to rearrange the furnitures and decorate the classrooms. Describe your plan in detail to the Chinese teacher of the school.

- 你为学生俱乐部设计了一件会员的T–恤衫。描述这件T–恤衫是什么样子：上面写着什么、画着什么、有些什么颜色或图案。

  You have designed a T-shirt for your student club. Describe to your club president (played by your teacher) what this T-shirt looks like, and give details about the text and positioning, colors, lines, and images.

- 你在一个中国公司工作，你向上司建议推销产品的一些想法，具体说明产品广告或网页的设计。

  While working for a Chinese company, you present to your boss ideas for marketing products. Specify the design of an advertisement poster or a webpage. Give details.

U1-4.5 语段写作：描述房间的原状和改变

Paragraph Writing: Write a descriptive paragraph based on the following situation. You are expected to present the scene spatially, using appropriate directional/locative phrases, verbs, and structures.

你到中国留学去的时候，你的一个朋友住在你的房间里。你从中国回来的时候，发现你的房间的样子完全变了：墙的颜色、窗帘、家具、地毯、桌子，甚至你的床单都变了。写两个段落。第一段描述你走以前的房间是什么样子（状态描述），第二段描述你朋友做的改变（行为及结果），并在描述时加上自己的看法。

When you studied in China, your room was used by a friend of yours. When you returned, you found your room drastically changed, e.g., the color of the walls, the curtain, the furniture, rug, table, and even your bed sheet. Write two paragraphs. Paragraph 1 describes what your old room was like (state). Paragraph 2 describes the changes your friend made (actions and results). Add necessary comments as you describe the state or results.

第
一
单
元
·
描
述
物
体
特
征

谈论物品特点
TALKING ABOUT PRODUCTS

第 一 课
Lesson 1

物品种类
TYPES OF PRODUCTS

 U2-1.2 词句操练 Aural-Oral Drills

There are **three** drills in this lesson, which can be completed in one session (*20 min.*). You need to complete each drill twice to achieve intended results.

Important note: Before starting each drill, be sure to preview the glossary for an initial familiarization with the new words and expressions to be covered (*follow the glossary number as indicated in each drill*). For best results, also type the new words between or after the two rounds.

U2-1.2-A 物品种类 ［词汇 U2.2］
看图听读, 并回答问题
Listen to each question carefully and answer it based on the given picture. In the second round, repeat each question before answering it.

1. 这里有哪一类的**物品**: **生活用品**、**食品**、**电子产品**？
2. 这些东西是哪一个**种类**的：**学生用品**、**家电产品**？
3. 这个地方有没有**食品**？有**电子产品**吗？
4. 这里有什么**产品**、**设备**：**电子产品**、**体育用品**？
5. 这里有什么**产品**、**设备**：**电子产品**、**体育用品**？

U2-1.2-B 器具、设备 ［词汇 U2.3］
看图听读, 并回答问题
Listen to each question carefully and answer it based on the given picture. In the second round, repeat each question before answering it.

1. 这些**产品**叫什么？是哪一类的**产品/设备**：**电子**还是**电器**？
2. 这几件东西叫什么?是哪一类的**产品/设备**：**电子**还是**电器**？
3. 这里有些**工具**。你觉得这些**工具**有用吗？
4. 这里有一些**餐具**。这些**餐具**是西式的还是中式的？
5. 这里有些什么**雨具**？有没有雨伞、雨衣、雨鞋？
6. 这套**家具**是什么式的：中式的、日式的，还是西式的？

U2-1.2-C 谈谈自己
Answer the following questions about yourself without pausing the audio clip. You have only a few seconds to answer each of them. In the second round, read each question aloud and answer it again. Be prepared to interview your classmates with these questions.

1. 你小时候喜欢什么？**电视机**、**玩具**，还是**电子游戏机**？
2. 你一般喜欢在哪里买**文具**：学校的书店还是一般的**文具店**？
3. 你最常用的**雨具**是什么？雨伞还是雨衣？
4. 你喜欢用中式**餐具**（如：碗、筷子）还是西式餐具（如：盘子、刀、叉）？
5. 学校开学的时候你需要买什么物品？
6. 第一次搬到学校去住，需要买一些什么用品？

7. 现在你房间里有些什么**家具**？

8. 现在你房间里有**哪些设备**？

9. 上一次你过生日的时候你收到的礼物是哪方面的：生活用品、学习用品、电子产品、还是别的？

10.下一次你过生日的时候，你希望收到哪方面的礼物？

流利强化 Fluency Enhancement

 U2-1.7 语块练习：用品、用具 [词汇 U2.0-2.3]

Chunking Exercise: First read each phrase out loud, and then type the phrase. For output efficiency and accuracy, type in words or phrases without breaking it down to single syllables. Be sure to check your Chinese characters for accuracy after each phrase is entered. For best results, also write the phrases by hand to improve your character reading and writing.

1. 用品和用具，　电子产品，　电器产品，　学习用品/用具，　生活用品/用具，　办公用品
   yòngpǐn hé yòngjù　diànzǐchǎnpǐn　diànqìchǎnpǐn　xuéxíyòngpǐn / yòngjù　shēnghuóyòngpǐn / yòngjù　bàngōngyòngpǐn

2. 中式家具，　西式餐具/厨具，　很方便的工具，　各种各样的文具，　很有意思的玩具
   zhōngshìjiājù　xīshìcānjù / chújù　hěnfāngbiànde gōngjù　gèzhǒnggèyàngde wénjù　hěnyǒuyìsìde wánjù

3. 需要买很多文具，　几张彩色的纸，　几支彩色的笔，　两把剪刀，　几个透明的文件夹
   xūyào mǎi hěnduōwénjù　jǐzhāng cǎisède zhǐ　jǐzhī cǎisède bǐ　liǎngbǎjiǎndāo　jǐgè tòumíngde wénjiànjiā

4. 这里有很多家具和用品，　深色的衣柜，　浅色的餐桌，　深红色的茶几，
   zhèlǐ　yǒuhěnduō jiājù　hé yòngpǐn　shēnsède yīguì　qiǎnsède cānzhuō　shēnhóngsède chájī
   很漂亮的落地灯
   hěnpiàoliangde luòdìdēng

5. 这里有一些雨具，　一把红色的雨伞，　一件绿色的雨衣，　一些大大小小的雨鞋
   zhèlǐ yǒu　yìxiēyǔjù　yìbǎ　hóngsède yǔsǎn　yíjiàn　lǜsède yǔyī　yìxiē　dàdàxiǎoxiǎode yǔxié

6. 餐具和厨具，　大大小小的碗和盘子，　一把刀子和叉子，　几双筷子，　一个很大的锅
   cānjù hé chújù　dàdàxiǎoxiǎode wǎnhépánzi　yìbǎdāozi　hé chāzi　jǐshuāngkuàizi　yígè　hěndàde guō

7. 家电产品和设备，　白色的冰箱，　黑色的微波炉，　不太大的洗衣机，
   jiādiànchǎnpǐn hé shèbèi　báisède bīngxiāng　hēisè　wēibōlú　bútàidàde　xǐyījī
   很大的彩电/彩色电视机
   hěndàde　cǎidiàn / cǎisè　diànshìjī

8. 生活用品，　需要一些日用品，　这是生活必需品，　那些是奢侈品，　需要一些装饰品
   shēnghuóyòngpǐn　xūyào　yìxiē rìyòngpǐn　zhèshì shēnghuó bìxūpǐn　nàxiē shì shēchǐpǐn　xūyào　yìxiē zhuāngshìpǐn

9. 学习用品，　旅行用品，　体育用品和设备，　办公用品和设备，　电子产品，　电脑设备
   xuéxíyòngpǐn　lǚxíngyòngpǐn　tǐyùyòngpǐn hé shèbèi　bàngōngyòngpǐn hé shèbèi　diànzǐchǎnpǐn　diànnǎoshèbèi

10. 很不错的照相机/相机，　很贵的手机，　很好玩的游戏机，　全新的洗衣机
    hěnbúcuòde　zhàoxiàngjī / xiàngjī　hěnguìde shǒujī　hěnhǎowánde yóuxìjī　quánxīnde　xǐyījī

第二单元 · 谈论物品特点

U2-1.8 速读/巩固：《送什么礼品？》 (5分钟)

Speed Reading/Review: Follow the steps below.

1. Read the passage "送什么礼品？" in Lesson 1 within <u>five</u> minutes, focusing on meaning. You are expected to understand the main ideas and recognize the core vocabulary items covered.

2. Without looking at the book, try to recall the gift types mentioned in the passage. Test yourself by categories such as gifts for children, women, men, seniors, weddings, and hosts.

3. Read or listen to the entire passage one more time, focusing on sentence connections and transitions.

 U2-1.9 流利练习：介绍礼品 （5分钟）

Fluency Drill: Listen to or read the paragraph below sentence by sentence. After you hear or read each sentence, pause for two to three seconds, and then say the whole sentence aloud from memory. You should repeat each sentence until you can read the sentence aloud smoothly and accurately. Long sentences are separated by lines for appropriate grouping.

一般来说，到别人家里去做客|都会带点东西。因为中国人特别喜欢酒，所以|最常见的礼品|就是包装得很漂亮的|名酒、红酒。另外，现在人们|也喜欢|对健康有好处的|食品、用品，如比较好的茶叶、装有各种水果的果篮|都是不错的选择；也可以给主人家的孩子或老人|送适合他们的东西。

第 二 课　**材料与规格**
Lesson 2　MATERIALS AND SPECIFICATIONS

 U2-2.2 词句操练 Aural-Oral Drills

There are <u>six</u> drills in this lesson, which can be completed in one session (*30 min.*). You need to complete each drill twice to achieve intended results.

Important note: Before starting each drill, be sure to preview the glossary for an initial familiarization with the new words and expressions to be covered (*follow the glossary number as indicated in each drill*). For best results, also type the new words between or after the two rounds.

U2-2.2-A 材料 [词汇 U2.5]
看图听读, 并回答问题
Listen to and read the questions while looking at the picture(s). Then answer the questions using one of the forms/expressions provided. In the second round, repeat each question before answering it.

> 看上去像……的; 可能是/有……; 我想不是/没有……的; 应该是/有……的

1. 这个手机是<u>什么材料(做)</u>的? 是不是**塑料**的?　→　看上去<u>不像塑料</u>的, 可能是……
2. 这些东西<u>是什么做</u>的? 是**陶瓷**的还是**塑料**的?
3. 这里有很多玻璃杯和塑料杯, 也有**陶瓷**的茶杯吗?
4. 这块桌布是<u>什么料子</u>的? 是**棉布**的还是**塑料布**的?
5. 这个窗帘<u>看上去不像丝绸</u>的, 是什么料子的?
6. 这个电脑包是<u>什么做</u>的? 是**真皮**的吗?
7. 这些箱子<u>用了哪些材料</u>? 这几个包呢?
8. 这些东西里有哪些材料?
9. 这些东西是什么做的?
10.这个书架上用的是**塑料板**还是**木板**?
11.哪些材料比较**硬**、哪些比较**软**? 哪些比较**光滑**?

U2-2.2-B 比喻用法 [词汇 U2.6]
Restate each sentence without changing the original meaning using the alternative form, as shown in the example.

> (X)V着(软)得像Y一样/似的　→　(X)V着像Y一样(软)

例：这种布料<u>摸着**软**</u><u>像羊毛一样/似的</u>。→ 这种布料<u>摸着像羊毛一样软</u>。
1. 这种塑料<u>摸着**硬**</u>得<u>像石头</u>似的。　→
2. 这个桌面<u>摸着**光滑**</u>得<u>像玻璃</u>一样。　→
3. 这种布料<u>看着**细腻**</u>得<u>像丝绸</u>似的。　→
4. 这种塑料板<u>看着**透明**</u>得<u>像玻璃</u>一样。　→

U2-2.2-C 面积、体积、长度 [词汇 U2.7]

Review the two forms below. Then listen to each question and answer it based on the information provided.

> 尺寸是多少? 有多大?

Form A: ……的尺寸有X厘米长（宽、高、厚）。

Form B: 长（宽、高、厚）X厘米。

Note: Form A is more common than Form B in conversations.

1. 这块木板的尺寸是多少？ (length = 200cm, width = 60cm, thickness = 2cm)

2. 这张桌子的尺寸是多少？ (length = 2 m, width = 1.2m, height = 1.5m)

3. 这块桌布有多大（尺寸是多少）？ （5英尺 × 7英尺）

4. 这个行李箱有多大（尺寸是多少）？ （26英寸 × 14英寸 × 9英寸）

> 面积/体积有多大? 是多少?

1. 这个房间的面积是多少？有多少平方米？ （10米 × 5米 = 50平方米）
   这个房间长10米，宽5米，有 50平方米。

2. 这个东西的体积是/有多少？ （4米 × 3米 × 2米 = 24立方米）

3. 这个圆桌的直径是多少？半径呢？ （130厘米；65厘米）

U2-2.2-D 重量、容量 [词汇 U2.8]

Review the two forms below. Then listen to each question and answer it based on the information provided.

> 重量是/有多少? 容量是/有多少?

Form A: 这个东西有 X 公斤（重）。

Form B: 这个东西重X 公斤。

Note: Form A is more common than Form B in conversations.

1. 那个电脑有多重/那个电脑的重量是多少？ （5lb/磅）

2. 那个电视机有多重/那个电视机的重量是多少？ （10kg/公斤）

3. 这个瓶子可以装多少酒？这个瓶子的容量是多少？ （500ml/毫升 ）

4. 这个瓶子可以装多少水？这个瓶子的容量是多少？ （4l /升）

U2-2.2-E 包装、容器 [词汇 U2.9]

听读并回答问题

Note the form of *measure words*: containers and vessels are nouns and can also be used as measure words.

1. 这些包装箱是纸的。　　　　→　　这些包装箱是什么做的？

2. 这个纸箱是装电脑的。　　　→　　这个箱子是什么做的？ 是装什么的？

3. 这个盒子里装了两瓶酒。　　→　　这个盒子里装了什么？

4. 这个塑料盒可以装文具。　　→　　这个盒子是什么做的？ 可以装什么？

5. 这里有两个装礼物的盒子。　→　　这里有什么？

6. 这里有两盒礼物。　　　　　→　　这里有多少礼物？

7. 这里有三个纸箱子。　　　　→　　这里有什么？

8. 这里有三箱纸。　　　　　　→　　这里有多少纸？

U2-2.2-F 谈谈你身边的东西

The following are questions about you or the items in your room. You are expected to answer each of them within a few seconds. In the second round, repeat each question before answering it. Be prepared to interview your classmates with these questions.

1. 你的书桌的体积大不大？ 尺寸是多少？ (有多少厘米/英寸？)

2. 你的书架是什么材料做的？ 有多高？ 是什么颜色？

3. 你的电脑体积有多大？ 重量是多少？ 有多厚？ (有多少厘米/英寸？)

4. 你喜欢体积大的电脑还是体积小的？

5. 你房间里有这些东西吗: 塑料管、木板、塑料板、金属杆、木杆、塑料杆？

6. 你房间里有哪些容器: 如塑料盒、纸箱、玻璃瓶、塑料盆、瓷盘等？

7. 过去两年里你收到过／送过一些什么样的礼物？ 请描述这些礼物的体积、重量和包装。 （如: 包装用的盒、纸、袋子; 材料、颜色、形状）

流利强化 Fluency Enhancement

 U2-2.9 语块练习：材料与规格 [词汇 U2.4-2.9]

Chunking Exercise: First read each phrase aloud, and then type it out. For output efficiency and accuracy, type in words or chunks instead of each character individually. Be sure to check your Chinese characters for accuracy after each phrase is entered.

1. 陶瓷笔筒， 玻璃盘子， 玻璃瓶， 塑料瓶， 大理石桌子， 木头架子
   táocíbǐtǒng bōlipánzi bōlipíng sùliàopíng dàlǐshízhuōzi mùtoujiàzi

2. 银餐具， 不锈钢厨具， 塑料文具， 塑料雨具， 木料家具， 塑料玩具
   yíncānjù búxiùgāng chújù sùliàowénjù sùliàoyǔjù mùliàojiājù sùliàowánjù

3. 化纤的桌布， 真皮沙发， 米色的真皮沙发， 帆布箱子， 有格子花纹的帆布箱子
   huàxiānde zhuōbù zhēnpíshāfā mǐsède zhēnpíshāfā fānbùxiāngzi yǒugézihuāwénde fānbùxiāngzi

4. 像羊毛一样软， 软得像羊毛一样， 光滑得像丝绸一样， 硬得像石头一样
   xiàngyángmáo yíyàngruǎn ruǎnde xiàngyángmáoyíyàng guānghuáde xiàngsīchóuyíyàng yìngde xiàngshítouyíyàng

5. 一块塑料板， 一块金属板， 一根塑料管， 一根橡皮管， 一根铁丝， 一根塑料绳
   yíkuài sùliàobǎn yíkuài jīnshǔbǎn yìgēn sùliàoguǎn yìgēn xiàngíguǎn yìgēntiěsī yìgēn sùliàoshéng

6. 3米长的橡皮管， 1尺宽的纸板， 5磅重的电脑， 10公斤重的箱子
   sānmǐchángde xiàngpíguǎn yìchǐkuānde zhǐbǎn wǔbàngzhòngde diànnǎo shígōngjīnzhòngde xiāngzi

7. 粗粗细细的铁丝， 长长短短的塑料绳， 宽宽窄窄的金属板， 高高矮矮的木架子
   cūcūxìxìde tiěsī chángchángduǎnduǎnde sùliàoshéng kuānkuānzhǎizhǎide jīnshǔbǎn gāogāo'ǎiǎide mùjiàzi

 U2-2.10 速读/巩固：《2008年北京奥运会的奖牌》

Speed Reading/Review: Follow the steps below.

1. Read the passage "2008年北京奥运会的奖牌" in Lesson 2 within two minutes, focusing on meaning. Without looking at the book, recall the descriptions of the medal design as described in the passage. Answer the questions.

2. Check the description (Paragraph 2) again to see how the original text was composed.

3. Read or listen to the entire passage one more time, focusing on sentence connections and transitions.

 U2-2.11 流利练习：奥运会奖牌（5分钟)

Fluency Drill: Listen to the following passage sentence by sentence. After each sentence, pause for two to three seconds, and then say the whole sentence aloud from memory. You should repeat a sentence until you can say it aloud smoothly and accurately. Long sentences are separated by lines for appropriate grouping.

2008年北京奥运会的奖牌|和以前的奖牌不一样：除了金、银、铜以外，还用了三种颜色的玉，这是奥运史上|第一次用了金属以外的材料|来做奖牌。听说这次奥运会|用了一吨的黄金和白银，还有3000块玉石。和别的奥运会金牌相比，北京奥运的金牌设计|很有中国特点。金牌直径是70毫米，厚度是6毫米。正面有一个图案，反面镶着一块玉，玉的中间|还有一个金属的|奥运会的会徽。金牌上用的玉|是白玉，和黄金放在一起|看上去很有特色。

U2-2.12 写作练习：描述一件礼物（10分钟)

Writing Exercise: Describe a commercial item (日用品、文具、电子产品、体育用品等) that can make a good gift. Provide as much information as you can to help the reader visualize the item including item type, color, shape, material, and any other specifications such as wrapping or packaging.

U2-2.13 词语自测：物品种类；材料与规格（5–10分钟)

Test yourself on the words and expressions in these categories: **materials**, **dimensions**, **weight**, **volume**, **capacity**, and **packaging**.

Suggestions:

1. **English-to-Chinese:** Use the English glossary of each section, covering the Chinese characters. Say each item aloud in Chinese as you read it in English. Mark the ones you fail to reproduce in Chinese for review (*you may also use flashcards*).

2. **Chinese-to-English:** Reverse the above to work on comprehension and character recognition. Mark the difficult characters for extra review.

3. **Memory Test:** Time yourself for three minutes and try to reproduce as many vocabulary items in the categories listed above as possible. You can type the items out in pinyin so that you don't lose count. When your time is up, go over the same sections in the vocabulary glossary to see what you have missed. Then test yourself again to improve your performance.

第 三 课 **介绍产品特点**
Lesson 3 PRODUCT INFORMATION

U2-3.2 词句操练 Aural-Oral Drills

There are <u>eight</u> drills in this lesson, which can be completed in two sessions (*A to D for session 1, and E to H for session 2, 30 min. each*). You need to complete each drill twice to achieve intended results.

Important note: Before starting each drill, be sure to preview the glossary for an initial familiarization with the new words and expressions to be covered (*follow the glossary number as indicated in each drill*). For best results, also type the new words between or after the two rounds.

U2-3.2-A 物体特性 [词汇 U2.10a, 2.10c]
听读句子并回答问题
Listen to and read the questions. Then choose the appropriate answer(s) from the list provided. In the second round repeat each question before answering it.

1. 水的温度变化会让水变成哪些形态? （液体、晶体、固体、气体）
2. 平常吃的**盐**(salt) 和**糖**(sugar)可以是什么样子的? （液体、晶体、固体、粉末）
3. **醋**(vinegar)闻着有什么味? （臭味、酸味、酒味）
4. 哪些材料闻着会有气味? （金属、塑料、橡胶、陶瓷、玻璃）
5. 这些材料里哪一个**摸着**不太**坚硬**? （玻璃、金属、塑料、皮革、陶瓷）
6. 这些材料里哪几种**摸着柔软**? （棉布、丝绸、塑料、陶瓷、橡胶）
7. 哪种材料可以**硬得像**石头**一样**，也可以**软得像**丝绸**一样**? （玻璃、金属、塑料、皮革、陶瓷）
8. 这个东西**看着/摸着**有什么特点? （柔软/坚硬、光滑/粗糙）
9. 这种料子**摸着**有什么特点? （柔软/坚硬、光滑、细腻/粗糙）
10.和丝绸比起来，帆布**摸着**有什么特点? （柔软/坚硬、光滑、细腻/粗糙）

U2-3.2-B 听读并回答问题: 防–、 易–、 耐– [词汇 U2.10b]
This drill works on the usage of three commonly used **prefixes**, and each has five to six questions for you to answer. In the second round, repeat each question before answering it.

防–
1. 一般来说，哪些材料是**防水**的? （说三种）
2. 哪些金属材料会**生锈**，哪些是**防锈**的?
3. **防水**的材料常用来做什么用品/用具? （如：日用品、办公用品、餐具、玩具、雨具）
4. 什么颜色常用来代表**防水物品**? （如：红色、黄色、绿色）
5. 什么材料**防腐**，做成的物品不会**腐烂**? （说三种材料）

易–
1. 哪些材料做的用具**易碎**? **易燃**? **易爆**?
2. 哪个不是**易碎品**：玻璃杯、塑料杯、陶瓷杯?
3. 哪种衣料**易燃**：棉布、丝绸、皮革、化纤、帆布?

4. **易燃**、**易爆**的东西常会是什么体的：固体、液体、气体？

5. 你的房间里有没有**易碎品**、**易燃品**？

6. 为了安全，什么**物品**一般不能带上飞机？

耐–；很耐–

1. 哪些材料**耐高温**？**耐酸**？**耐腐蚀**？

2. 哪些用具/用品特别需要有**耐高温**的性能？**耐酸/耐腐蚀**性能？

3. 哪种材料做的物品更**耐磨**：皮革、化纤、塑料、金属？

4. 哪种衣料最**不耐磨**：棉布、帆布、皮革、丝绸？

5. 哪一类的物品应该买**耐用**的：文具、餐具、工具、电子产品、家电……

U2-3.2-C 性能、功能、用途 ［词汇 U2.10］

转换句式

Listen to and repeat each sentence while reading the text, and then restate the sentence using the form or expression provided.

1. 塑料<u>防水</u>、<u>防腐</u>。 → （有……的<u>性能</u>）

2. 不锈钢可以<u>防锈</u>、<u>耐高温</u>。 → （有……的<u>性能</u>）

3. 这个手机也可以<u>上网</u>、<u>听音乐</u>、<u>玩游戏</u>。 → （有……的<u>功能</u>）

4. 这个数码相机<u>可以做很多事情</u>。 → （有很多<u>功能</u>；<u>功能</u>很多）

5. 这种材料<u>可以用来做很多东西</u>。 → （有多种<u>用途</u>；<u>用途</u>很多）

6. 在日用品方面，这种材料<u>很有用</u>。 → （有很大的<u>用途</u>；<u>用途</u>很大）

U2-3.2-D 做比较 ［词汇 U2.10］

回答问题

Listen to and repeat each question while reading the text, and then answer it using the word(s) or form(s) provided. Note the comparative expressions and forms. See Appendix 1 in the Textbook for English meanings of the comparative expressions.

比较常用词语句式

Familiarize yourself with these expressions used for stating an opinion and/or making a comparison. See Appendix 1 for the glossary.

1. 在我看来；对我来说；我觉得；我认为……

2. 在防水性能方面；从防水性能上看……

3. 和X比起来，Y的……

4. 在……方面，X和Y有同样的功能/用途；X和Y的功能/用途一样。

5. X有/没有……的性能/功能。

6. X的……性能/功能比Y 好；Y的……性能/功能不如X（好）。

7. X比Y的功能/用途更多；Y的功能/用途不如X的多。

比较不同材料

1. 金属有哪些<u>性能</u>? （耐—、 防—）
2. <u>和金属比起来</u>，塑料的哪些<u>方面</u>比较好? （耐—、防—、软/硬）
3. 因为塑料有很多性能，所以<u>用来做什么</u>最合适? （用来做—用品、—具、—机、—器）
4. <u>在哪些方面</u>，塑料<u>不如陶瓷</u>?
5. 在哪些性能方面，陶瓷<u>不如塑料</u>?
6. 为什么有的人喜欢用塑料餐具，有的人喜欢陶瓷和不锈钢餐具?
7. <u>相比之下</u>，木料的哪些性能、功能或用途不如塑料?

比较手机和电脑

1. 对你来说，<u>手机哪些功能</u>比较重要? （如: 打电话、发短信、上网、照相、听音乐、玩游戏、看电影……）
2. 对你来说，<u>手机最大的用途</u>是什么? （方便和别人通话、方便自己的各种需要）
3. 在你看来，<u>在哪些功能和用途方面</u>，手机不如电脑?
4. 电脑和手机都<u>有很多用途</u>，可是如果你只能有一个，你要电脑还是手机? 为什么?

U2-3.2-E 外观、表面、质地 (形容词) ［词汇 U2.13］

Listen to and read each question while looking at the picture, and then answer the question. In the second round, repeat each question before answering it.

看图回答问题

1. 在你看来，这款手机的式样够不够**新颖**? 够不够**美观**?
2. 这个沙发的面料看着怎么样? (很**软**/硬、很**细腻**/粗糙、很结实、很美观、很舒适)
3. 这个家具有什么特点? (美观、新颖、光滑、轻便、笨重、结实)
4. 这些塑料餐具**看着**很像什么材料的? 你想，**摸着**也像吗?
5. 在你看来，这张桌子怎么样? (比较……；不够……；非常……)
6. 以前手机(大哥大)在**体积**和**外观**上怎么样? **功能**呢?
7. 和以前的手机相比，现在的手机有什么特点?

U2-3.2-F 分辨词义 ［词汇 U2.13］

用哪个词?

For each item, answer the question with the appropriate word from the list provided.

1. 摸着很**光滑**的东西，**质地**应该怎么样? （结实、细腻、轻便、坚硬、粗糙 ）
2. 很多**轻便**的物品和什么有关? （新颖、柔软、小巧、美观、舒适）
3. 哪些特点用手**摸**一下就知道? （轻便、光滑、软/硬、细腻/粗糙、舒适）
4. 一般来说，哪些物品**闻着**<u>没有</u>**气味**? （金属、橡胶、皮革、塑料、陶瓷）
5. 如果你把塑料放在火上，**闻着**会有一股什么**味**? （香味、臭味、酸味、橡胶味）

U2-3.2-G 成语、常用词组［词汇 U2.14］

改换说法：口语转书面语

This drill works on **adjectives** that describe products. For each item, listen to the sentence and then restate it using the expression(s) provided.

例：这个产品外观很简单，但很漂亮。　（美观大方）→ 这个产品美观大方。

1. 这个家具很结实、很耐用。　（结实耐用）

2. 这个电脑重量很轻，体积也很小。　（轻便小巧）

3. 这个石料看着又光滑又细腻。　（光滑细腻）

4. 这种餐具又好又便宜。　（物美价廉）

5. 这种产品的设计很新、很特别。　（款式新颖）

6. 这几件东西其实是冒牌货。　（伪造产品/假冒产品）

7. 这是质量非常好的产品。　（优质产品）

8. 这里卖的手机有很多种。　（品种多样）

9. 这款手机什么功能都有。　（功能齐全）

10. 这个地方电子产品最多，什么都有。　（品种齐全、应有尽有）

11. 这是一个国际上有名的牌子。　（国际名牌/国际品牌）

U2-3.2-H　谈谈自己的物品

Answer the questions as if you were chatting with a Chinese friend. In the second round, repeat each question before answering it. Be prepared to interview your classmates with these questions.

1. 你用的是一个什么电脑？（什么牌子、型号、哪国制造的）

2. 你觉得这个牌子和型号的电脑有哪些好的特点？
   (如：款式新颖、美观大方、轻便小巧、结实耐用、物美价廉……)

3. 你认为你以前的电脑哪些方面不够好？
   (如：外观不够美观、功能不够齐全、体积不够轻便小巧、质量不够好、价格太高……)

4. 你买电脑的时候比较看重什么？（如：外观、性能功能、耐用、质量、体积、牌子）

5. 你买手机第一看重的是什么？（如：物美价廉、款式新颖、名牌产品、功能齐全）

6. 你买衣服的时候比较看重什么？（如：牌子、舒适、款式、价格、质量、结实）

7. 你买家具的时候比较看重什么？（如：牌子、舒适、款式、价格、质量、结实）

流利强化 Fluency Enhancement

U2-3.10 语块练习

Chunking Exercise: Type out each phrase twice as you read it aloud. The longer sentences have been broken down into shorter chunks. You are expected to get 100% accuracy. Long sentences are separated by lines for appropriate grouping.

U2-3.10-A 描述、比较物品特性 [词汇 U2.10-2.13]

1. 对我来说，在我看来，我认为，我觉得

2. 很耐用，很耐磨，不耐高温，不防水，防水性能，防腐性能，耐火材料，易燃品

3. 在防水性能方面，从防水性能上看，在手机的功能方面，从手机的功能上看

4. 和金属比起来，和金属相比，和塑料比起来，和塑料相比

5. 有同样的功能，有上网的功能，有玩游戏的功能，有很多功能和用途

6. 这个手机的上网功能|比那个的好，那个手机的上网功能|不如这个。

7. 这个洗衣机的功能|不如那个， 这个电脑的功能|不如那个的多。

8. 这种材料的用途|比那种材料的多，这种材料的用途|不如那种材料。

9. 摸着比较柔软，摸着不够坚硬，摸着非常光滑细腻，摸着有点粗糙

10. 闻着有一股(gǔ)味，闻着有一股塑料味，闻着有臭味/香味/酸味，闻着很臭/很香/很酸

U2-3.10-B 常用四字词组 [词汇 U2.14]

1. 这个产品美观大方， 这个家具结实耐用， 这个电脑轻便小巧
   zhègèchǎnpǐn měiguāndàfāng   zhègèjiājù   jiēshinàiyòng   zhègèdiànnǎo qīngbiànxiǎoqiǎo

2. 这种石料看着光滑细腻， 这种餐具物美价廉， 这种产品款式新颖
   zhèzhǒngshíliào kànzhe guānghuáxìnì   zhèzhǒngcānjù   wùměijiàlián   zhèzhǒngchǎnpǐn kuǎnshìxīnyíng

3. 这些都是伪劣产品， 这个不是假冒产品， 这个是国际名牌， 质量很好/是优质产品
   zhèxiēdōushì wěilièchǎnpǐn   zhègèbúshì   jiǎmàochǎnpǐn   zhègèshì guójìmíngpái   zhìliànghěnhǎo / shì yōuzhìchǎnpǐn

4. 这里的手机品种多样， 这款手机功能齐全， 这里电子产品品种齐全、应有尽有
   zhèlide shǒujī pǐnzhǒngduōyàng   zhèkuǎnshǒujī gōngnéngqíquán   zhèli diànzǐchǎnpǐn pǐnzhǒngqíquán yīngyǒujìnyǒu

第 三 课 · 介 绍 产 品 特 点

U2-3.11 语句练习：谈物品性能、功能

Read each sentence aloud, pause for <u>two</u> seconds, repeat the sentence, and then type it out. Be sure to check your Chinese characters for accuracy after each sentence is entered. Long sentences are separated by lines for appropriate grouping.

1. 这个手机|也有上网、听音乐、玩游戏的功能。

2. 这个数码相机|有很多功能。

3. 这种材料|有多种用途。

4. 在日用品方面，这种材料|有很大的用途。

5. 在我看来，塑料用来做日用品|最合适。

6. 他认为，和金属比起来，塑料的防水性能比较好。

7. 在耐热性能方面，塑料|不如陶瓷和金属。

8. 温度的变化|可以让水|变成气体和固体。

9. 在高温下，塑料闻着|会有一股臭味。

10. 对他来说，手机的上网功能|不重要。因为在他看来，手机的最大用途|是方便和别人通话。

U2-3.12 模仿朗读：《大减价买什么？》 (5分钟)

Play back the first half of the dialogue in Lesson 3 in the textbook, sentence by sentence. Pause to repeat each sentence and mimic the speech and tone of the speakers. You may also choose to play the role of the husband or the wife in this dialogue.

U2-3.13 写作练习：描述一件产品 (5–10分钟)

Writing Exercise: Describe a commercial product. Provide information about its make and specifications. Comment on its design and quality using the vocabulary and expressions you have learned recently. Remember to support a general comment with specific details.

U2-3.14 词语自测：介绍产品特点 （5分钟）

Vocabulary Self-Testing: Test yourself on the words and expressions in this lesson, using the translation or flashcard method (**English-to-Chinese** or **Chinese-to-English**), or the timed memory test method. Remember, even just a few minutes will effectively help you retain your vocabulary items for a much longer time.

第 四 课 Lesson 4	**比较物品** COMPARING PRODUCTS

U2-4.3 语段示例

Read the additional sample paragraphs through once, paying special attention to **sentence connections** and **transitions**. Also note the use of **punctuation marks** (*e.g., commas are used between sentences within a subtopic*). Then listen to the clip and read it again for the feel of the sentence flow and transitions.

语段示例 1

描述手机	款 kuǎn	(measure word)

我刚买了一款手机。我原来的手机轻便小巧，款式不错，可是屏幕不够大。新买的这款手机外壳是银色的，屏幕表面是黑色的，非常光滑。因为是高清大屏幕，所以画面非常清晰，看着舒服多了。在功能方面，这款手机比别的款式更齐全，不但可以照相、上网、发短信、听音乐，而且还可以玩游戏、看电影、录音，等等。另外，竖着用横着用都非常方便。从价格上看，这种多功能大屏幕手机比一般型号的贵得多，但用着更方便！总的来说，这款手机给人的感觉是美观大方，功能齐全！如果你也想换手机，我建议你试试这种款式。

屏幕 píngmù	screen, monitor
外壳 wàiké	casing
表面 biǎomiàn	appearance
高清 gāoqīng	high definition (HD)
画面 huàmiàn	images displayed on the screen
照相 zhàoxiàng	to take pictures
录音 lùyīn	audio recording
竖着 shùzhe	vertically
横着 héngzhe	horizontally
建议 jiànyì	to suggest; to recommend

语段示例 2

比较行李箱	

这个行李箱比那个好多了。虽然从款式上看，这个箱子不如那个新颖，但这个的材料比那个好得多，而且还有防水、耐火的性能，所以相比之下更结实耐用。从体积上看，那个箱子是更小巧一点，颜色也比较漂亮，所以女人会比较喜欢。而这个的款式比较适合男人。总的来说，和很多名牌产品比起来，这个牌子的行李箱的质量一点也不差，但价格却便宜得多，可以说是物美价廉。

行李箱 xínglǐxiāng	suitcase
差 chà	poor, low in quality
便宜 piányi	cheap

单元测试与报告 Unit Assignments

For the unit review and assignments, please consult Appendices 1-3 for a guide on language use, grammar, and discourse structure.

U2-4.4 词语测试：本单元词语句式及语言结构

Vocabulary Test: Review the words and expressions in this unit and prepare for a unit test.

U2-4.5 口头报告：介绍公司产品

你的工作面试里有一项任务是向客户介绍公司的产品：比较产品的外观、款式、体积、性能、功能和用途; 说明质量档次、价格、售后服务。

Oral Task: Your job interview includes a scenario of marketing your product to Chinese customers. Present a product by comparing it to similar items, and convince your customers that your product is not only superior in quality but also affordable, with excellent after-sales service and product support.

U2-4.6 语段写作：退换物品；推荐产品 (20 分钟)

Paragraph Writing: Complete one of the following simulation tasks within 20 minutes.

- 你是客户，写信给客服中心，抱怨你对买的物品不满意，做详细描述和比较，要求退换(tuìhuàn / exchange) 或退款 (tuìkuǎn / refund)。

  You are a customer filing a complaint to a Customer Service about something you purchased online. Describe the discrepancies between the item you received and the one advertised. Request for an exchange or refund.

- 你买了一件产品后发现非常好，所以写信给你的朋友推荐这个产品。描述产品，并与同类产品做比较。

  You like a product you bought recently. Write an email to your friend recommending the product. Describe this product and compare it with similar products.

活动程序和要求 Guidelines and Instructions for the Tasks

1. 阅读讨论活动要求 Guidelines for the Reading and Discussion Activities

Your good preparation for and active participation in the class discussions are required. Follow the instructions below (unless otherwise specified by your instructor).

For reading texts: All students are expected to read each text before scheduled in-class discussions. Be prepared for answering comprehension questions in class. Jot down notes if you find a difference between Chinese culture and your own, and be ready to share your observation in the class discussion. Use a notebook or flashcards to collect useful words and expressions from the reading passages.

For your assigned task: If you have been assigned a text to lead a class discussion activity (by yourself or your group), you (or your group) should also prepare your activity by following these guidelines:

1) Your activity should last at least <u>five</u> minutes.
2) Keep your activity steps simple, clear, and efficient; do not try to accomplish too many things!
3) Limit your new vocabulary terms, if any, to five. Write the new terms on the blackboard to facilitate comprehension.
4) Have your outline, procedure, or script checked by your teacher in advance.

2. 文化手工体验与交流
Follow your teacher's instructions on cultural experience with arts and crafts.

3. 作文/课堂报告
Follow the directions below to prepare your projects.

a. 介绍一件和文化有关的物品 Introducing a Cultural Product

内 容 Content	介绍一件与你熟悉的文化有关的物品，如手工艺品、饰品、或有特别象征意义的用具等。描述主要特征特点，如颜色、形状、体积、性能、用途等;介绍这个物品的意义、象征、风俗习惯等。 Introduce a traditional product in the culture you are familiar with, such as a handicraft article, jewelry, or a tool or utensil that bears a special meaning or symbolism. Provide detailed descriptions of the product's main features, e.g., color, shape, size, other traits, and use. Also provide brief information on the meaning, symbolism, and cultural practices related to this product.
作 文 Essay	写一篇350字的短文，适当加入图片；宋体或仿宋体，字号12，行距为2 (或按照老师的要求);交给老师以前，请先检查汉字。 Write an essay with 350 characters and add appropriate images if necessary. Use the Song or Fangsong font for Chinese, 12 points, with double-line spacing (unless otherwise specified by your teacher). Be sure to check your characters for accuracy before submission.
口头报告 Presentation	用幻灯投影方式在课上做介绍，介绍的最后部分包括测试题，提问其他同学。（报告中不能念作文或稿子，但可以在幻灯片里提示关键词语）。报告时间：5-8分钟。 Prepare a slide presentation. Include quiz questions at the end for audience participation. Note that you may not read from your essay or script, but you are allowed to include key words in your slides as hints. Time limit: 5-8 minutes.

Use the worksheet below to prepare the details of a cultural item. Consult **Appendix** for useful phrases.

文化/国家	
物品名称	
特征/特点 颜色、形状、 质地、体积等	
用 途	
象征意义	

b. 介绍一件产品 （选一个情景）
Introducing a Commercial Product or an Object (Choose one of the following scenarios)

内 容 Content	情景1：推销产品，描述特征特点（外部特征、规格、性能、功能、用途等），说明产品质量、售后服务等,适当与同类产品做比较。 **Scenario 1:** Market a product; describe its main features (physical design and specifications, traits, function and use); comment on its quality, after-sales service etc, and compare it to other similar products.
	情景2：介绍一种想象的产品（如：未来的……）；描述特征特点（外部特征、规格、性能、功能、用途等），说明产品质量、售后服务等，并与同类产品做比较。 **Scenario 2:** Introduce an imagined item (e.g., a future product...). Describe its main features (physical design, appearance and specifications, traits, function and use); comment on or project its quality, after-sales service etc, and compare it to other similar products. Be sure to review U2-L5 for the paragraph organization and discourse structure. Incorporate appropriate comparative expressions and transitional phrases (also see the handout for comparative expressions).
口头报告 Presentation	准备用幻灯投影的方式在课上报告。报告的最后部分要回答观众问题。（不能念稿子或用卡片提示，但可以用幻灯片提示关键词语）。报告时间: 6–8分钟。 Prepare a slide presentation. Include a brief Q & A interaction with the audience at the end of presentation. **Note** that you are not allowed to read from your script or use index cards, but you are allowed to include key phrases in your slides as hints. Time limit: 6-8 minutes.

Use the worksheet below to prepare the details of your presentation on a commercial or imaginary item. See Appendices 2 and 3 in the Textbook for your production guide.

产品名称/型号	
材料	
体积/尺寸	
重量	
颜色	
质地	
款式	
性能、功能	
用途	
价格	
其他特点	
比较其他产品	

Useful comparative and transitional phrases (See **Appendix 1** in the Textbook)

_____   _____

_____   _____

_____   _____

第三单元

UNIT **3**

描述人物印象
DESCRIBING PEOPLE

第 一 课 | **生理特征**
Lesson 1 | PHYSICAL FEATURES

 U3-1.2 词句操练 Aural-Oral Drills

There are **four** drills in this lesson, which can be completed in one session (*25 min*). You need to complete each drill twice to achieve intended results.

Important note: Before starting each drill, be sure to preview the glossary for an initial familiarization with the new words and expressions to be covered (*follow the glossary number as indicated in each drill*). For best results, also type the new words between or after the two rounds.

U3-1.2-A 生理特征 [词汇 U3.0-3.2]
听读，并回答问题

For each item, listen to the question and answer it. In the second round, repeat each question before answering it.

1. 这里有几个<u>什么人</u>?　　　　　　　　（青少年、中年妇女、青年男/女子）

2. 这个人是什么<u>个子</u>?　　　　　　　　（中等个、瘦高个、高个、大个、小个）

3. 你想，这个小伙子<u>身高</u>和<u>体重</u>是多少?　（1米8, 85公斤；　5英尺7英寸, 170磅）

4. 这两个女的<u>身材</u>怎么样?　　　　　　（长得很苗条、丰满、单薄、瘦小、健壮）

5. 这两个人是什么<u>体型</u>?　　　　　　　（长得比较高大、矮小、健壮、单薄）

U3-1.2-B 面部特征、头发、发型 [词汇 U3.3-3.4]
听读, 并回答问题

For each item, listen to the question and answer it. In the second round, repeat each question before answering it.

1. 这个姑娘是什么<u>脸型</u>? 她长着一张瓜子脸、鹅蛋脸，还是苹果脸?

2. 这个小伙子是什么<u>脸型</u>? 长脸、方脸、长方脸还是圆脸?

3. 这个姑娘<u>留着长发还是短发</u>?

4. 这个小伙子<u>长着一头黑发还是一头卷发</u>?

5. 这个人面部有<u>什么特征</u>? （<u>长着一个宽额头、尖下巴、有一颗痣</u>……）

U3-1.2-C 其他特征 [词汇 U3.5]
回答问题

Listen to the questions and answer them. In the second round, repeat each question before answering it.

1. 这个人有什么特征? （看上去像东方/西方人、＿＿＿＿＿洲人）

2. 哪个人<u>看上去像亚洲人</u>? （长着/留着＿＿＿＿＿发的那个）

3. 这个中年妇女<u>有外国口音</u>，她可能是哪国人? （看上去像＿＿＿＿＿国人）

U3-1.2-D 谈一个自己熟悉的人

Answer the following questions based on a person you are familiar with.

1. 这个人是什么性别? （男性、女性）
2. 他/她是什么年龄的人? （儿童、青少年、年轻人、中年人、……）
3. 他/她是哪里人? （北美、亚洲、欧洲、非洲、……）
4. 这个人是什么个子? （高个、中等个、瘦高个、矮胖个、……）
5. 你想他/她的身高差不多是多少? （有1米75、有5英尺5）
6. 你想他/她的体重差不多是多少? （有X公斤/磅）
7. 他/她是什么身材/体型? （长得很高/矮、健壮、苗条、……）
8. 他/她长着什么样的头发? （黑发、黄发、卷发、……）
9. 他/她留着什么发型? （长发、短发、小平头、……）
10. 他/她是什么脸型? （圆脸、长方脸、椭圆脸、……）
11. 他/她有什么面部特征? （浓眉毛、大眼睛、高鼻子、尖下巴、……）
12. 他/她说话带有什么口音? （南方/北方、_____国、……）

流利强化 Fluency Enhancement

 U3-1.8 语块练习：人物外部特征 [词汇 U3.0-3.4]

Chunking Exercise: First read each phrase aloud, and then type the phrase. For best result, also select some phrases to write by hand.

1. 矮胖个，   瘦高个，   中等个，   身高1米75，   体重80公斤
   ǎipànggè   shòugāogè   zhōngděnggè   shēnggāo yìmǐqīwǔ   tǐzhòng bāshígōngjīn

2. 年轻人，   中年人，   老年人，   年轻姑娘，   中年妇女
   niánqīngrén   zhōngniánrén   lǎoniánrén   niánqīnggūniang   zhōngniánfùnǚ

3. 瘦高的年轻小伙子，   很苗条的年轻姑娘，   很健壮的中年男性
   shòugāode niánqīngxiǎohuǒzi   hěnmiáotiaode niánqīng gūniang   hěnjiànzhuàngde zhōngniánnánxìng

4. 矮矮胖胖的中年妇女，   瘦瘦小小的老头，   高高大大的外国人
   ǎiǎipàngpàngde   zhōngniánfùnǚ   shòushòuxiǎoxiǎode lǎotóu   gāogāodàdàde   wàiguórén

5. 长着一张圆脸，   一双大眼睛，   长着一头黑亮的头发，   长着一个宽额头
   zhǎngzhe yìzhāngyuánliǎn   yìshuāngdàyǎnjīng   zhǎngzhe yìtóu hēiliàngde tóufà   zhǎngzhe yígè kuān'étóu

6. 留着披肩发，   留着短发，   留着小胡子，   留着小平头，   剃了个光头
   liúzhe pījiānfà   liúzhe duǎnfà   liúzhe xiǎohúzi   liúzhe xiǎopíngtóu   tìlegè guāngtóu

7. 脸上有一对酒窝，   额头左边有一颗痣，   脸上有一个疤/一条疤
   liǎnshàng yǒu yíduìjiǔwō   é'tóuzuǒbiān yǒu yìkēzhì   liǎnshàng yǒu yígèbā / yìtiáobā

8. 说话有口音，   说话有南方/北方口音，   说话有很重的外国口音
   shuōhuà yǒu kǒuyīn   shuōhuà yǒu nánfāng / běifāngkǒuyīn   shuōhuà yǒu hěnzhòngde wàiguókǒuyīn

9. 圆圆的脸，   细长的眉毛，   尖尖的下巴，   黑黑的眼睛，   白白的皮肤
   yuányuánde liǎn   xìchángde méimao   jiānjiānde xiàba   hēihēide yǎnjing   báibáide pífū

U3-1.9 词语复习

Review the following *adjectives* and *nouns*. Then fill in the blanks with appropriate nouns. The first one has been done for you as an example.

形容词 *Adjectives*:

圆　　方　　尖　　厚　　薄　　浓　　粗　　细　　高　　长
yuán　fāng　jiān　hòu　báo　nóng　cū　xì　gāo　cháng

名词 *Nouns*:

皮肤　头发　额头　眉毛　眼睛　鼻子　嘴　嘴唇　下巴　个子　身材　声音　脸
pífū　tóufa　étóu　méimao　yǎnjing　bízi　zuǐ　zuǐchún　xiàba　gèzi　shēncái　shēngyīn　liǎn

圆　**脸、眼睛**　　　　　　浓 _____

方 _____　　　　粗 _____

尖 _____　　　　细 _____

厚 _____　　　　高 _____

薄 _____　　　　长 _____

细长的 _____　　白白的 _____

粗粗的 _____　　亮亮的 _____

瘦小的 _____　　红红的 _____

高大的 _____

黑黑的 _____

U3-1.10 速读/巩固：《理想的外表》(5分钟)

Speed Reading/Review: Follow the steps below.

1. You may listen to the passage "理想的外表" in Lesson 1 once before reading, if that works for you.

2. Read the passage within two minutes, focusing on meaning.

3. Without looking at the book, reflect on the main ideas and recall as many details as possible.

4. Read the entire passage one more time, focusing on the details.

5. Write down useful words and expressions for future review and practice.

U3-1.11 流利练习：描述人物特征 ［词汇 U3.0-3.4］ （5分钟）

Fluency Drill: Listen to or read the sentences below. After each item, pause for two to three seconds, and then say the sentences from memory.

1. 他是个20多岁的年轻人，长得高高大大的，剃了个光头。
2. 那个中年男性长着长方脸、浓眉毛，留着小胡子。
3. 那个姑娘看上去像个高中生，身材有点瘦小。她长着一张圆脸，脸上有一对酒窝。
4. 那个小伙子身高有1米75，体重差不多有90公斤，看上去很健壮。
5. 那个女的是个中年人，中等个，留着短发，嘴角边有一颗痣，说话有一点南方口音。
6. 这位女性个子1米65左右，身材很苗条。她留着长发，长着一张鹅蛋脸，一对细长的眉毛和一双黑黑的眼睛。

U3-1.12 词语自测：生理特征 （5分钟）

Vocabulary Self-Testing: Test yourself on the words and expressions in at least three of the following categories:

- Names for different ages and genders
- Height, build, weight, and figure
- General physical features and body parts
- Special facial features and hair style
- Verbs to describe different features or styles
- Measure words for physical features
- Other identifiable features of a person such as skin color, hair color, and accent

Suggestions:

1. **English-to-Chinese:** Use the English glossary of each section, covering the Chinese characters. Say each item aloud in Chinese as you read it in English. Mark the ones you fail to reproduce in Chinese for review (*you may also use flashcards*).

2. **Chinese-to-English:** Reverse the above to work on comprehension and character recognition. Mark the difficult characters for extra review.

3. **Memory Test:** Time yourself for three minutes and try to reproduce as many vocabulary items in the categories listed above as possible. You can type the items out in pinyin so that you don't lose count. When time is up, go over the same sections in the vocabulary glossary to see what you have missed. Then test yourself again to improve your performance.

第 二 课 | **穿着打扮**
Lesson 2 | APPAREL AND ATTIRE

 U3-2.2 词句操练 Aural-Oral Drills

There are <u>seven</u> drills in this lesson, which can be completed in two sessions (*A-D for Session 1, and E-G for Session 2, 20 min. each*). You need to complete each drill twice to achieve intended results.

Important note: Before starting each drill, be sure to preview the glossary for an initial familiarization with the new words and expressions to be covered (*follow the glossary number as indicated in each drill*). For best results, also type the new words between or after the two rounds.

U3-2.2-A 日常穿着 [词汇 U3.6-3.11]

跟读

This drill works on the terms for clothing: **types of clothing**, **associated measure words** and **verbs**. Repeat the words or phrases as you hear it.

名词

1. **套装：**西服/装、休闲装、运动服
2. **上装：**外衣、毛衣、T-恤衫、衬衫、风衣
3. **下装：** 裤子、牛仔裤、裙子
4. **鞋袜：**鞋、靴子、袜子
5. **帽子：**安全帽、棒球帽

量词

1. **套：** 一套西服/装、休闲装、运动服
2. **件：** 一件外衣、毛衣、T-恤衫、衬衫、风衣
3. **条：** 一条裤子、牛仔裤、裙子
4. **双：** 一双鞋、靴子、袜子
5. **顶：** 一顶帽子

动词

1. **穿着**一套西服/装、休闲装、运动服
2. **穿着**一件外衣、毛衣、风衣、衬衫
3. **穿着**一条长裤、 牛仔裤、 短裙
4. **穿**一双运动鞋、高跟鞋、皮鞋、 靴子、袜子
5. **戴着**一顶帽子、棒球帽

U3-2.2-B 形容颜色、形状、式样 [词汇 U3.7-3.11]

用所给的词语回答问题

First review the listed descriptive phrases. Then answer the questions using the phrases provided.

> 深灰色的　浅蓝色的　鲜红色的　花花绿绿的　带条纹的

例：他穿着一套什么样的西装？(深灰色的)　　→　他穿着一套深灰色的西装。

1. 他**穿着**一条什么样的裤子？　(浅蓝色的；短裤)　→

2. 她**穿着**一双什么样的鞋？　(鲜红色的；高跟鞋) →

3. 她**穿着**一条什么样的裙子？　(花花绿绿的；长裙)→

4. 他**穿着**一件什么样的衣服？　(带条纹的；衬衫)　→

5. 他**戴着**一顶什么样的帽子？　(白色的；棒球帽)　→

U3-2.2-C 饰品、佩戴物品 [词汇 U3.12]

跟读

This drill works on **clothing items**, associated *measure words* and *verbs*. Repeat the word or phrase as you hear it.

名词

1. 领带、围巾、皮带、手套、眼镜、项链、耳环、手表

量词

1. 一**顶**帽子；一**条**领带、皮带、围巾；一**副**眼镜

2. 一**双**手套；一**只**手表；一**对**耳环；一**串**项链

动词

1. **戴着**一顶帽子、一双手套、一副眼镜、一只手表、一串项链、一对耳环

2. **系着**一条领带、一条皮带

3. **围着**一条围巾

U3-2.2-D 谈谈自己的穿着喜好

First review the listed materials. Then answer the following questions about your preferences on clothing. In the second round, repeat each question before answering it.

> 衣料：　棉布　　丝绸　　真皮　　羊毛　　化纤
> 　　　　miánbù　sīchóu　zhēnpí　yángmáo　huàxiān

1. 你现在穿着什么样的衣服, 比方说：衬衫、T-恤衫、毛衣、外套，等等？

2. 夏天你喜欢穿什么样的衣服？冬天呢？

3. 你觉得什么料子做的衣服比较舒服, 比方说：棉布、丝绸、真皮、羊毛、化纤，等等？

4. 你喜欢戴帽子吗？什么样的帽子？是什么做的？

5. 你最喜欢穿什么鞋？是什么牌子的？哪国出产的？

6. 你喜欢用哪些饰品和佩戴物品，比方说领带、围巾、皮带、项链、耳环、手表，等等？

7. 在你自己的国家，工作面试的时候一般应该穿什么样的服装比较合适？

8. 在你自己的国家，穿什么样的衣服去上课或者去上班不合适？比方说：

凉鞋 (sandals)、超短裙 (miniskirt)、短裤 (shorts)？

9. 如果你的中国朋友刚到你们国家来，现在要去参加学校的欢迎晚会，认识很多人，你觉得他/她应该怎么打扮自己？穿中式服装还是西式服装？如果去你家呢？

U3-2.2-E 形容打扮 [词汇 U3.6-3.12]

用所给的词语回答问题

First review the listed descriptive phrases. Then answer the questions using the phrases provided.

> 带紫色条纹的　花花绿绿的　很宽的　银色的　棕色的　细长的　形状特别的

例：他系着一条什么样的领带？（带紫色条纹的）　→　他系着一条带紫色条纹的领带。

1. 她围着一条什么样的围巾？ （花花绿绿的）　→

2. 她系着一条什么样的皮带？ （很宽的、红）　→

3. 他带着一副什么眼镜？ （宽边的、太阳镜）→

4. 她戴着一串什么样的项链？ （银色的）　→

5. 他戴着一双什么样的手套？ （棕色的、真皮）→

6. 她戴着一对什么样的耳环？ （细细长长的）　→

7. 他戴着一只什么样的手表？ （形状很特别的）→

U3-2.2-F 身体部位与穿戴物品

This drill works on a common form that describes a person's appearance by using a body part as the topic. First repeat the sentence. Then listen to the question and answer it based on the given information. In the second round, refrain from looking at the text.

> 头 (head)　脖子 (neck)　身 (body)　手 (hand)　脚 (foot)
> tóu　　　bózi　　　 shēn　　 shǒu　　　jiǎo

跟读　　　　　　　　　　　　　回答问题

1. 那个中年妇女头上戴着一顶帽子。　→　那个中年妇女头上戴着什么？

2. 那个老头手上戴着一副皮手套。　→　那个老头手上戴着什么？

3. 那个姑娘脖子上围着一条白色的围巾。→　那个姑娘脖子上围着什么？

4. 那个小伙子脚上穿着一双运动鞋。　→　那个小伙子脚上穿着一双什么鞋？

5. 那个年轻人身上穿着一套西装。　→　那个年轻人身上穿着什么衣服？

U3-2.2-G 动作状态与携带物品 [词汇 U3.13]

This drill works on common verbs used with "着" to describe the state of a person carrying items. Again, body parts are used as the topic. See "Forms and Structures" in the Textbook for notes and usage examples.

拿	拎	提	挎	背	抱	顶
ná	līn	tí	kuà	bēi	bào	dǐng

For each item, listen to the initial sentence and note the **verb** used. Then answer the question <u>in a complete sentence</u> based on the given information.

听读原句		回答问题
1. 那个小伙子手里**拿着**一个钱包。	→	那个小伙子手里**拿着**什么？
2. 那个姑娘手里**拎着**一个小箱子。	→	那个姑娘手里**拎着**什么？
3. 这个男的肩上**挎着**一个电脑包。	→	这个男的肩上**挎着**什么？
4. 这个学生背上**背着**一个书包。	→	这个学生背上**背着**什么？
5. 那个人头上**顶着**一个箱子。	→	那个人头上**顶着**什么？

流利强化 Fluency Enhancement

U3-2.7 语块练习：穿着打扮 [词汇 U3.6-3.13]

Chunking Exercise: First read each phrase/sentence aloud, and then type it out. Select some phrases to write by hand.

1. 一件黑大衣， 一件厚厚的黑大衣， 他穿着一件厚厚的黑大衣
   yíjiàn hēidàyī　　yíjiàn hòuhòude hēidàyī　　tāchuānzhe yíjiàn hòuhòude hēidàyī

2. 一条长裙， 一条花花绿绿的长裙， 她穿着一条花花绿绿的长裙
   yìtiáo chángqún　　yìtiáo huāhuālǜlǜde chángqún　　tāchuānzhe yìtiáo huāhuālǜlǜde chángqún

3. 一套浅色的西服， 一套漂亮的浅色西服， 他穿着一套漂亮的浅色西服
   yítào qiǎnsède xīfú　　yítào piàoliangde qiǎnsèxīfú　　tāchuānzhe yítào piàoliangde qiǎnsèxīfú

4. 穿着一件带格子的衬衫， 穿着一双黑亮的皮鞋， 穿着一双红色的高跟鞋
   chuānzhe yíjiàn dàigézide chènshān　　chuānzhe yìshuāng hēisède píxié　　chuānzhe yìshuāng hóngsède gāogēnxié

5. 一条丝绸围巾， 一条花花绿绿的丝绸围巾， 她围着一条花花绿绿的丝绸围巾
   yìtiáo sīchóuwéijīn　　yìtiáo huāhuālǜlǜde sīchóu wéijīn　　tāwéizhe yìtiáo huāhuālǜlǜde sīchóu wéijīn

6. 一条带条纹的领带， 一条带红色条纹的领带， 他系着一条带红色条纹的领带
   yìtiáo dàitiáowénde lǐngdài　　yìtiáo dàihóngsètiáowénde lǐngdài　　tājìzhe yìtiáo dàihóngsètiáowénde lǐngdài

7. 一顶帽子， 一顶黑色的礼帽， 他戴着一顶棒球帽
   yìdǐngmàozi　　yìdǐng hēisède lǐmào　　tādàizhe yìdǐng bàngqiúmào

8. 一串项链， 一串银项链， 一对金耳环， 她戴着一对金耳环
   yíchuànxiàngliàn　　yíchuàn yínxiàngliàn　　yíduì jīn'ěrhuán　　tādàizhe yíduì jīn'ěrhuán

9. 戴着一双黑手套， 戴着一块名牌手表， 戴着一副宽边眼镜， 系着一条很细的皮带
   dàizhe yìshuāng hēishǒutào　　dàizhe yíkuài míngpái shǒubiǎo　　dàizhe yífù kuānbiān yǎnjìng　　jìzhe yìtiáo hěnxìde pídài

10. 拿着一个钱包， 拎着一个手提包， 提着一个电脑包， 抱着一些书， 背着一个书包
    názhe yígè qiánbāo　　līnzhe yígè shǒutíbāo　　tízhe yígè diànnǎobāo　　bàozhe yìxiēshū　　bēizhe yígè shūbāo

U3-2.8 描述练习：我看到的嫌疑犯 （10分钟）

Describing a Suspect: Describe the two people in the pictures. Provide as many details as possible about the person's physical features, clothing, and accessories.

Photo courtesy of David Reed Thomas

Photo courtesy of Tony Cheung

U3-2.9 写作练习：描写人物外表 （10分钟）

Writing Exercise: Write about a person you saw or met recently detailing **physical features**, **clothing**, and **accessories**.

U3-2.10 词语自测：穿着打扮 （5分钟）

Memory Test: Time yourself for five minutes and see how many words and expressions (with *measure words*) you are able to reproduce orally. Name clothing items for…

1. different seasons: e.g., winter, summer, etc.
2. a job interview (male, female)
3. a formal party (male, female)
4. a vacation at the beach
5. a dance party (male, female, accessories and jewelry)

第三单元 · 描述人物印象

第 三 课 ┃ **人物印象**
Lesson 3 ┃ DESCRIBING IMPRESSIONS
OF A PERSON

 U3-3.2 词句操练 Aural-Oral Drills

There are <u>six</u> drills in this lesson, which can be completed in two sessions (*A-D for Session 1, E-F for Session 2, 20 min. each*). You need to complete each drill twice to achieve intended results.

Important note: Before starting each drill, be sure to preview the glossary for an initial familiarization with the new words and expressions to be covered (*follow the glossary number as indicated in each drill*). For best results, also type the new words between or after the two rounds.

U3-2.2-A 形容长相/相貌 [词汇 U3.14]
根据提示替换词语
This section works on adjectives and four-character set phrases together with the verb form "**长得**". Restate the sentence by replacing the underlined part of the sentence with the word/phrase provided. In your restatement, you must use the verb form "**长得**". Follow the example below.

> （那个人）长得……
>
> | 浓眉大眼/很帅 | 眉清目秀/很清秀 | 五官端正 | 相貌出众 | 相貌平平/不够英俊 |
> |---|---|---|---|---|
> | nóngméidàyǎn / hěnshuài | méiqīngmùxiù / hěnqīngxiù | wǔguānduānzhèng | xiàngmàochūzhòng | xiàngmàopíngpíng / búgòuyīngjùn |

例：他长着浓浓的眉毛, 大大的眼睛。（浓眉大眼/很英俊） → 他长得<u>浓眉大眼</u>; 他长得<u>很英俊</u>。

1. 那个姑娘长着细长的眉毛和眼睛。 （眉清目秀/很清秀） →

2. 提着公文包的那个人<u>长得还不错</u>。 （五官端正） →

3. 戴眼镜的那个男生<u>长得很一般</u>。 （相貌平平/不够英俊）→

4. 那个小伙子<u>长得很帅</u>。 （相貌出众/很英俊） →

U3-3.2-B 形容穿着打扮 [词汇 U3.15]
根据提示替换词语
Restate each sentence using "**不够**" and the word provided.

> | 一般/讲究 | 随便/正式 | 俗气/素雅 | 时髦/保守 | 开放/古板 |
> |---|---|---|---|---|
> | yìbān / jiǎngjiū | suíbiàn / zhèngshì | súqì / sùyǎ | hímáo / bǎoshǒu | kāifàng / gǔbǎn |

例：那个瘦高个穿得有一点随便。 （正式）→ 那个瘦高个穿得<u>不够正式</u>。

1. 身材很苗条的那个女孩穿得比较<u>俗气</u>。（素雅）→

2. 那位男士穿得非常<u>一般</u>。 （讲究）→

3. 那个年轻姑娘穿得太<u>古板</u>了。 （开放）→

4. 那个中年妇女穿得特别<u>保守</u>。 （时髦）→

U3-3.2-C 形容性格特点和言谈举止 [词汇 U3.17]

This drill works on adjectives that describe people's character traits. First review the *adjectives* below which are paired with their *antonyms*. Then follow the example shown below to start the drill.

外向/内向	热情/冷淡	活泼/文静	合群/孤僻	风趣/严肃	细心/粗心
wàixiàng / nèixiàng	rèqíng / lěngdàn	huópo / wénjìng	héqún / gūpì	fēngqù / yánsù	xìxīn / cūxīn

Restate each sentence with an *antonym* using this form: 不是一个＿＿＿＿的人

例：那个小伙子是一个性格外向的人。 （内向） → 那个小伙子不是一个内向的人。

1. 那个姑娘很活泼。 （文静） →
2. 那位女士有一点孤僻。 （合群） →
3. 这位男士非常风趣。 （严肃） →
4. 那个中年人非常圆滑。 （直爽） →
5. 那个年轻人做事有点粗心。 （细心） →
6. 那位先生有点冷淡。 （热情） →

U3-3.2-D 意思相关的形容词 [词汇 U3.17]

This drill helps you memorize commonly associated *adjectives*. Review the *adjectives* below and then follow the example for the drill.

外向—热情大方	腼腆—文静	傲慢—冷淡	单纯—直爽	严肃—深沉
wàixiàng rèqíngdàfāng	miǎntiǎn wénjìng	àomàn lěngdàn	dānchún zhíshuǎng	yánsù shēnchén

Add a **comment** with associated trait(s) using "他/她比较……", as shown in the example below. In the second round, say each sentence with added comment as a whole.

例：小刘是一个性格很外向的人。 （热情、大方） → 他比较热情、大方。

1. 小刘的女朋友有一点腼腆。 （文静） →
2. 那个王先生给人一种傲慢、自大的印象。 （冷淡） →
3. 那个年轻人给人的印象是很单纯。 （直爽） →
4. 那位老师给人一种很严肃的感觉。 （深沉） →

U3-3.2-E 表达人物印象：素质与特点 [词汇 U3.18]

This drill works on making comments with "有-phrases". Respond to the following questions or statements using the forms and expressions provided, as shown in the examples.

> ……是一个_____的人

1. 戴着眼镜的那位男士怎么样？ （很有礼貌） → 他是一个很有礼貌的人。
2. 穿着大衣的那位老先生怎么样？ （很有学问） →
3. 长得眉清目秀的那个男孩子怎么样？ （很有教养） →
4. 穿得很时髦的那个女的怎么样？ （很有才干） →

> 其实(他/她)是一个_____的人

1. 穿着短裙的那个姑娘长得太矮。 （很有能力） → 其实她是一个很有能力的人
2. 那个年轻女子看上去很时髦。 （非常没有教养） →
3. 戴着帽子的那位女士长得相貌平平。 （很有才干） →
4. 拎着公文包的那个人对人很冷淡。 （很有见解） →

U3-3.2-F 表达人物印象：言谈举止 (复习[词汇 U3.17])

This drill reviews adjectives of character traits while working on two common expressions for describing impressions of people. For each item, read the initial sentence and complete the second part by using the words provided, as shown in the examples. In the second round, say each item in its entirety fluently.

> ……, 看上去很(有点、比较、非常、特别)_____

1. 那个小伙子是一个比较外向的人，…… （非常活泼） → 看上去非常活泼
2. 这个年轻姑娘不够大方，…… （有点腼腆） →
3. 那个时髦的女性非常傲慢，…… （特别冷漠） →

> ……, 说起话来很(有点、比较、非常、特别)_____

1. 那位男士虽然相貌平平，但…… （非常风趣） → 但说起话来非常风趣
2. 那个青少年比较浅薄，而且…… （特别粗俗） →
3. 这位中年妇女非常热情，而且…… （比较幽默） →

流利强化 Fluency Enhancement

 U3-3.8 语块练习

Chunking Exercise: Read each phrase or sentence aloud. Then type the phrase or sentence with 100% accuracy.

U3-3.8-A 形容外表 [词汇 U3.14-3.15]

1. 英俊， 长得很英俊， 那个男的长得不够英俊
   yīngjùn　　zhǎngde hěnyīngjùn　　nàgènánde zhǎngde búgòuyīngjùn

2. 长得浓眉大眼、五官端正， 这个小伙子长得浓眉大眼、五官端正
   zhǎngde nóngméidàyǎn　wǔguānduānzhèng　zhègè xiǎohuǒzi zhǎngde nóngméidàyǎn　wǔguānduānzhèng

3. 清秀， 长得很清秀， 这个小姑娘长得很清秀
   qīngxiù　　zhǎngde hěnqīngxiù　　zhègè xiǎogūniang zhǎngde hěnqīngxiù

4. 眉清目秀， 长得眉清目秀， 那个女生长得眉清目秀
   méiqīngmùxiù　　zhǎngde méiqīngmùxiù　　nàgènǚshēng zhǎngde méiqīngmùxiù

5. 相貌平平， 相貌出众， 这个人看上去相貌平平， 他的女朋友相貌出众
   xiàngmàopíngpíng　xiàngmàochūzhòng　zhègèrén kànshàngqù xiàngmàopíngpíng　tāde nǚpéngyǒu xiàngmàochūzhòng

6. 穿得很随便， 穿得很讲究， 打扮很得体， 打扮得很俗气
   chuānde hěnsuíbiàn　chuānde hěnjiǎngjiu　dǎban hěndétǐ　dǎbande hěsúqi

7. 穿得很古板， 穿着一套很古板的衣服， 穿着一件土里土气的衣服
   chuānde hěngǔbǎn　chuānzhe yítào hěngǔbǎnde yīfu　chuānzhe yíjiàn　tǔlǐtǔqìde　yīfu

8. 看上去很得体， 打扮得不够得体， 看上去穿得很讲究
   kànshàngqù hěndétǐ　dǎbande búgòudétǐ　kànshàngqù chuānde hěnjiǎngjiū

U3-3.8-B 描述印象 [词汇 U3.16-3.18]

1. 性格外向， 他性格比较外向， 性格很内向， 是一个性格比较内向的人
2. 有点严肃， 看上去有点严肃， 非常热情大方， 看上去非常热情大方
3. 比较冷淡， 给人的感觉是很冷淡， 给人一种冷淡的感觉
4. 很自信， 特别自信， 不够自信， 给人的印象是不够自信
5. 很幽默， 很风趣， 说起话来很风趣， 他给人一种幽默风趣的感觉
6. 很成熟， 比较成熟， 不够成熟， 她给人的印象是不够成熟
7. 很活泼， 特别活泼， 不够活泼， 很傲慢， 很自大， 给人一种傲慢的感觉
8. 很浅薄， 有点浅薄， 不够深沉， 他给人一种浅薄、不够深沉的感觉

第三单元・描述人物印象

U3-3.9　速读/巩固：《小王的第一印象》 (5分钟)

Speed Reading/Review: Follow the steps below.

1. You may choose to listen to the story "小王的第一印象" in Lesson 3 once before reading, if it works for you.
2. Read the story within three minutes, focusing on meaning. When you finish, reflect on the main ideas and recall as many details as possible.
3. Read the entire story one more time, focusing on the details.
4. Write down useful words and expressions for future review and practice.

 U3-3.10 流利练习：描述人物特征 (5分钟)

Choose a paragraph from Part Two of the story "小王的第一印象". Listen to it sentence by sentence. After each sentence, pause for two seconds, and then say the whole sentence aloud from memory. You should repeat the sentence until you can say it smoothly and accurately. Continue the exercise to finish the paragraph.

> 　　几次通话以后，小王好像已经能清楚地看见对方了：鹅蛋脸，眉清目秀，长长的、黑黑亮亮的披肩直发；身材很苗条，爱穿一件素雅的衬衫，或者是一件色调柔和的毛衣，下身穿一条……牛仔裤？不对不对，还是长裙更像一点。咳，不管是牛仔裤也好，还是长裙也好，反正她穿着都好看，可能有点保守，但还是让人感觉很美……
>
> 　　好不容易等到了约会的那一天，小王满面春风，心情愉快，眼睛里充满了兴奋和希望。他平时穿得总是比较随便，T-恤衫、牛仔裤就行了，头发也总是乱乱的。可今天他特别打扮了半天。"第一次见面一定得给对方一个好印象！"他这么想。于是他穿上平常很少穿的黑色西装，系上一条带条纹的领带，皮鞋擦得亮亮的，乱乱的头发也梳得顺顺的，马上就变得面目一新！小王高高兴兴地出去约会了……

U3-3.11 写作练习：表达印象 （10分钟）

Writing Exercise: Choose one of the following scenarios for this writing exercise:

1. Imagine you are Xiao Wang in the story "小王的第一印象". Write to your best friend about the date. Describe the girl you imagined over the phone and the girl you met in person. Express your feelings (disappointment, excitement, etc.).
2. Imagine you are Xiao Wang's date. Write to your best friend about the date. Tell him/her about the Xiao Wang you imagined over the phone and the guy you met in person. Express your feelings (disappointment, excitement, etc.).
3. Imagine you dated a person for a few weeks and decided to stop seeing him/her. Write to your Chinese teacher/friend commenting on this person's strengths and weaknesses, and the reason for your decision.

Requirements: Discuss the person's looks, the way the person was dressed, his/her manners, and your impressions or feelings. Support your general comments with specific descriptions and examples.

Useful Phrases and Expressions

1. 我原来以为他/她……，可是……　　　　I had thought that he/she…, but it turned out…
2. 见面后(我)发现他/她……　　　　　　　When we met in person, I found that he/she…
3. 哪知道他/她其实……　　　　　　　　　To my surprise, he/she actually…
4. 奇怪的是/有意思的是……　　　　　　　What is weird/funny is that …
5. 我对他/她感到很满意/失望　　　　　　　I was/am happy/disappointed with him/her.

［满意 (mǎnyì: happy with) 失望 (shīwàng: disappointed)］

第三课 · 人物印象

第 四 课 | 描绘人物
Lesson 4 | PORTRAYING A PERSON

U3-4.3 语段示例

Listen to and then read the sample paragraphs in this lesson in the Textbook, paying special attention to paragraph organization and topic transitions. Also note the use of punctuation marks. Then choose one paragraph to do the fluency or typing exercise.

人物特点描述

The following is an additional descriptive writing sample for reading and practice. Give specific details appealing to the senses and use analogies or exaggerations to help evoke pictures in the mind of the reader.

一个奇怪的男人

　　这个饭馆里最近总是出现一个奇怪的男人，今天他又来了，身上穿着一件棕黑色的皮夹克和一条半旧的牛仔裤，脚上穿着一双特大号的运动鞋。他长得特别健壮，身高差不多1米90，体重至少也有120公斤！他剃个光头，亮得好像在黑屋子里也能闪闪发光。他的皮肤有点红中带黑，眉毛看不太清楚，不知是本来长得就很少还是剃头时顺便给剃光了。这样一来他的眼睛看上去就显得又圆又大又亮，亮得好像有火一样，让人看了有点害怕。奇怪的是，他的脸上总是没有什么表情，从来不笑，嘴巴也闭得紧紧的，好像只有吃饭说话时才愿意张开。他说话时声音很粗也很低沉，如果去唱歌一定会是个不错的男低音。不过他不开口还好，一开口就满口粗话。这个大汉每天都到这个餐馆来，一个人坐在那儿喝酒，脸上冷冰冰的。奇怪，他到底是个什么人？

用生动化比喻及夸张用法来描述人物外表细节及言谈举止。

Sketch of a person with descriptions of physical appearance and manner, analogies with moderate exaggerations.

单元测试与报告 Unit Assignments

For the unit review and assignments, please consult Appendices 1-3 for a guide on language use, grammar, and discourse structure.

U3-4.4 词语测试：本单元词语句式及语言结构

Vocabulary Test: Review the words and expressions in this unit and complete the online or written test assigned by your teacher.

U3-4.5 模拟任务：比较印象；介绍朋友

Role Play: Work in pairs to prepare and present the following scenarios. Use the "General to Specific" format (*or vice versa*) for your descriptions of a person. In addition, use sentence connectives and transitional phrases (*see Appendix 1 for a list of phrases*).

任务1：比较印象

(A角) 你在网上认识了一个人，几次聊天以后对对方的第一印象很不错，所以决定下网见面。结果见面以后发现这个人跟你原来想象的很不一样，而且并没有你想象的那么好。所以你和一个同学谈这件事，比较你的印象和感觉。谈得具体详细一点(长相、穿着、言谈举止等)。

任务2：介绍朋友

(B角) 你听了A的事情以后，觉得应该给他/她介绍两个很不错的朋友。你拿出照片来，做详细的介绍和比较(长相、穿着、言谈举止等)。

For Task 1: Use this table to prepare details. Consult the glossary in Appendix 1 for comparative expressions.

	在网上的感觉和你的想象	见面时的感觉和印象
个子		
身材/体型		
长相		
穿着		
言谈举止		
其他		
感觉、印象		

For Task 2: Find two photos (a male and a female) and use this table to prepare details of them.

	男 性	女 性
年龄		
个子		
身材/体型		
穿着打扮		
言谈举止		
其他		
给你的感觉、印象		

U3-4.6 语段写作：他/她怎么变成了这个样子?

Paragraph Writing: Describing and contrasting the **past and present** characteristics of a person

选一张人物图片做写作练习。想像这个人是你认识的一个人，如同学、朋友、亲戚等，然后描述你们第一次见面的时候他/她是什么样子，给你什么感觉和印象。现在他/她变成什么样子了? 描述这个人现在的外表、穿着打扮、言谈举止和给你的感觉。

Guidelines

1. Write two paragraphs describing and contrasting the past and present characteristics of a person. The person can be real or imaginary. Use a picture of a person for inspiration and include the picture(s) in your essay.

2. Use both general comments and specific descriptions. Organize your paragraphs using paralleled topic-comment structure, spatial order, as well as commonly used connectives and transitions. See the description examples in the Textbook and the following useful phrases.

3. Peer review. Have at least one classmate read your essay and provide comments. Revise and proofread before submitting it to your teacher.

Useful Phrases

In addition, also see the glossary of comparative expressions and transitional phrases in Appendix 1.

1. 我还清楚地记得我们第一次见面的情况。	I still remember our first meeting vividly.
2. 有意思的是……	Interestingly...
3. 我万万没想到的是……	What I could not possibly imagine was...
4. 真没想到，过了X年以后他/她……	Surprisingly, after X years he/she...
5. 我几乎认不出她/他来了。	I could barely recognize him/her. (几乎 jīhū: nearly, almost)
6. 我简直不敢相信……	I could hardly believe... (简直 jiǎnzhí: simply, virtually)

第三单元·描述人物印象

第四单元
UNIT **4**

介绍人物简况
INTRODUCING PEOPLE

第一课
Lesson 1

行业与职业
INDUSTRY AND
PROFESSION

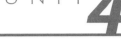

U4-1.2 词句操练 Aural-Oral Drills

There are <u>five</u> drills in this lesson, which can be completed in one session (*30 min*). You need to complete each drill twice to achieve intended results.

Important note: Before starting each drill, be sure to preview the glossary for an initial familiarization with the new words and expressions to be covered (*follow the glossary number as indicated in each drill*). For best results, also type the new words between or after the two rounds.

U4-1.2-A 熟悉领域名称 ［词汇 U4.1］

This section reviews common terms of fields and domains. Repeat each term as you hear it, looking at the characters. In the second round, memorize all the words.

_____领域　　_____界

1. 政治	2. 经济	3. 法律
4. 教育	5. 文学	6. 艺术
7. 历史	8. 体育	9. 医学
10. 新闻	11. 自然科学	12. 社会科学

U4-1.2-B 谈论各行各业 ［词汇 U4.0-4.1］

回答问题, 注意动词用法
Answer the following questions. **Note** the *verb* used in each question.

做/搞_____; 从事_____(方面的工作)

Note: "从事" is formal, and "搞" is colloquial. In Taiwan, "做" is used instead of "搞".

1. 你的亲戚朋友有没有搞政治、经济或者法律的?

2. 你认识的人里有没有搞文学、艺术、历史的?

3. 你想不想从事自然科学方面的工作?

4. 你觉得搞社会科学有没有意思?

5. 你对哪个领域比较感兴趣? (文学、艺术、自然科学等)

6. 在学校里你学过哪些方面的课? (文学、艺术、自然科学等)

U4-1.2-C 行业名称 [词汇 U4.2]

熟悉行业名称

This section reviews the common **terms for industry**. Repeat each term as you hear it, looking at the characters. In the second round, memorize as many terms as possible.

> ＿＿＿＿＿业 　　　＿＿＿＿＿行业
>
> **Note:** "业" or "行业" is often omitted except for monosyllabic words such as "工业", "农业", and "商业".
>
> 1. 工业　　　　2. 农业　　　　3. 商业　　　　4. 金融　　　　5. 食品
>
> 6. 制药　　　7. 汽车制造　8. 建筑　　　9. 网络　　　10. 信息
>
> 11. 美容　　　12. 旅游　　　13. 服务　　　14. 房地产　　15. 国际贸易/外贸

U4-1.2-D 谈论行业职业 [词汇 U4.0-4.2]

熟悉行业名称

This drill works on common **verbs** for expressing **professions**. Answer the following questions and note the verb usage.

> 他是搞/做什么的? 他以后想搞/做什么?

Note: "行业" or "业" is typically omitted when a disyllabic or polysyllabic word is used to avoid confusion.

例：他是搞什么的? 　　　　　　　　　(电脑)　　→　　　他是搞电脑的。

1. 小王以前是做什么的? 　　　　　　(建筑)　　→
2. 小张过去是不是搞房地产的? 　　(美容)　　→
3. 老李不搞房地产了，他现在想做什么? (外贸) →
4. 听说张先生改行了，他现在搞什么? (商业) →

U4-1.2-E 动词用法 [词汇 U4.0-4.2]

替换动词

This drill works on two common verb forms for expressing **professions or occupations**. Listen to each sentence, and then restate it using the substitute verb form, as shown below and in the first sentence.

> 搞/做＿＿＿＿＿　→　干＿＿＿＿＿这一行

例：小王以前是搞建筑的。 　→　小王以前是干建筑这一行的。

1. 小张过去是搞/做美容的。 →
2. 她姐姐想搞/做金融。 →
3. 她过去曾经搞/做过旅游。 →
4. 老李不搞/做房地产了。 →
5. 老李现在搞/做外贸了。 →

流利强化 Fluency Enhancement

 U4-1.7 语块练习：谈论行业、职业 [词汇 U4.0-4.2]

Chunking Exercise: First read each phrase aloud, and then type it out with 100% accuracy. Pinyin is not provided for this exercise.

1. 教育界，商界，金融界，法律界，然科学界，他在法律界有很多朋友

2. 制药业，汽车制造业，美容业，信息产业，服务业，网络广告业，旅游业

3. 他是搞教育的，他是做教育的，他以前是搞商业的，他没搞过商业

4. 搞教育/从事教育，搞政治/从事政治，不想从事经济，没从事过法律

5. 从事法律方面的工作，从事经济方面的工作，没从事过教育方面的工作

6. 干哪一行，干房地产这行，他是干建筑这行的，他不干建筑这行了

7. 改行搞别的，改行搞房地产，她不想搞金融了，想改行从事国际贸易

 U4-1.8 流利练习：表达行业、职业

1. 他朋友是搞金融的，在一家银行工作。

2. 她以前搞过教育，后来改行搞商业了。

3. 他以前没有干过电脑这一行，所以对电脑不感兴趣。

4. 她干过旅游这一行，所以应该对这一行的情况比较了解。

5. 他想学法律，以后从事法律方面的工作。

6. 过去10年中她一直从事国际贸易方面的工作，最近改行了。

7. 他以前从事过什么？今后想干哪一行？

8. 她认为应该从事自己最有兴趣的工作，而不是看什么行业最热门。

 U4-1.9 速读/巩固：《中国最热门的行业》（5分钟）

Speed Reading/Review: Follow the steps below.

1. You may choose to listen to the passage once before reading.

2. Read the passage within <u>three</u> minutes focusing on the main ideas.

3. When you finish the first round, recall as many details as possible. Try to name all top ten industries.

4. Read the entire passage one more time, focusing on the details.

5. Write down useful expressions for future review and practice.

U4-1.10 写作练习：谈论行业（5-10分钟）

Writing Exercise: Choose a few people you know (friends and family) and write about their occupations (past and present). Also write about your own career planning. Try to change **verb forms** (搞, 做, 从事, 干……这一行) in describing professions and occupations.

第一课·行业与职业

第 二 课   **身份与职务**
Lesson 2   IDENTITY AND POSITION

 U4-2.2 词句操练 Aural-Oral Drills

There are **five** drills in this lesson, which can be completed in one session (*30 min.*). You will need to complete each drill twice to achieve intended results.

Important note: Before starting each drill, be sure to preview the glossary for an initial familiarization with the new words and expressions to be covered (*follow the glossary number as indicated in each drill*). For best results, also type the new words between or after the two rounds.

U4-2.2-A 职业、身份 [词汇 U4.3]
用适当的名称完成下面的句子
Complete the following sentences by choosing the appropriate **occupation**. In the second round, read the complete sentence out loud.

1. 他是搞教育的，他是一个＿＿＿＿＿。

2. 她以前从事体育工作，她是一个＿＿＿＿＿。

3. 老张从事过新闻工作，曾经是一个＿＿＿＿＿。

4. 老王是搞艺术的，是一个很不错的＿＿＿＿＿。

5. 李先生是搞商业的，是一个大公司的＿＿＿＿＿。

6. 那位女士从事文学工作，是一个＿＿＿＿＿。

律师 lùshī	医师 yīshī	教师 jiàoshī	工程师 gōngchéngshī
推销员 tuīxiāoyuán	运动员 yùndòngyuán	演员 yǎnyuán	售货员 shòuhuòyuán
法官 fǎguān	记者 jìzhě	警察 jǐngchá	军人 jūnrén
科学家 kēxuéjiā	企业家 qǐyèjiā	作家 zuòjiā	画家 huàjiā
学者 xuézhě	推销员 tuīxiāoyuán	演员 yǎnyuán	官员 guānyuán
作家 zuòjiā	工人 gōngrén	职员 zhíyuán	会计师 kuàijìshī

U4-2.2-B 相关动词用法 [词汇 U4.0, 4.3]
This drill works on the **verbs** for describing **occupation** or **position**. Note the style for informal or formal usage.

替换动词
Listen to or read the original sentence, and then restate it with the substitute verb provided as shown in the first sentence.

> 当   做   担任

Note: "当" is colloquial and more common than "做". "担任" is formal and typically associated with an office appointment.

1. 小李以前做过公关人员。   (担任/当)   →   小李以前当过公关人员。

2. 小王以后很想做画家。   (当)   →

3. 她爸爸以前是一个演员。   (当过)   →

4. 她妈妈做过中学校长。   (担任/当)   →

5. 小李的男朋友想做建筑师。   (当)   →

```
干  搞  做  从事  +  (field/industry)
```

Caution: Never put the person's occupation, e.g., "演员", "公关人员", after these verbs.

1. 小李以前是<u>干</u>什么的?   (做/搞)   →   小李以前是<u>做</u>什么的?
2. 老张以前是<u>搞</u>电脑的。   (干电脑这一行)   →
3. 她以后想当老师，<u>搞</u>教育。   (从事)   →

U4-2.2-C 换一种说法 [词汇 U4.0-4.3]
Repeat the original sentence, and then restate it using two other forms below. Follow the example in the first sentence.

```
是一个_____    →    是搞/从事_____的; 是干_____这一行的
```

Pay special attention to the *verb* in each sentence form and make an effort to memorize the *verb-noun* collocations.

1. 他<u>是一个</u>运动员。   (体育)   →   他是<u>搞</u>体育<u>的</u>; 他是<u>干</u>体育<u>这一行的</u>。
2. 这位老先生<u>是一个</u>医生。   (医学)   →
3. 那个中年女性<u>是一个</u>画家。   (艺术)   →
4. 这个小伙子<u>是一个</u>作家。   (文学)   →
5. 那位男士<u>是一个</u>建筑师。   (建筑)   →

U4-2.2-D 语句扩展 [词汇 U4.0, 4.3, 4.4]
This drill works on expanding sentences with specifics. For each item, listen to the initial sentence, and then complete it with the information provided, as shown in the first sentence. In the second round, say the entire sentence aloud fluently.

```
是搞/从事_____的, 在一个_____里当_____
```

Note: "担任" is formal, normally used for special appointment or higher positions.

1. 她是<u>搞</u>教育<u>的</u>, ……   (学校; 老师)   →   她是<u>搞</u>教育<u>的</u>, <u>在一个</u>学校<u>里当</u>校长。
2. 他是<u>从事</u>法律<u>的</u>, ……   (地方; 法官)   →
3. 他朋友想<u>从事</u>新闻, ……   (电视台; 实习生)   →
4. 小李是<u>搞</u>房地产<u>的</u>, ……   (公司; 经理助理)   →
5. 老张是<u>从事</u>金融<u>的</u>, ……   (银行; 经理)   →

U4-2.2-E 谈谈自己

Imagine you are chatting with someone, and answer the following questions. Be prepared to do an interview with your classmates in class.

1. 你小时候想长大以后当什么？
2. 后来你的想法变了吗？想做什么了？
3. 现在你想干哪一行？
4. 为什么你想从事这方面的工作？
5. 你的家人和朋友希望你在哪方面发展？为什么？

流利强化 Fluency Enhancement

U4-2.8 语块练习：职业和身份 ［词汇 U4.3-4.4］

Chunking Exercise: Listen to or read each phrase aloud, and then type it out with 100% accuracy. For best results, also write all phrases by hand.

1. 当过教师，做过工程师，当过会计师，在一家公司当过工程师
2. 想当画家，不想当作家，想当科学家，不想当文学家
3. 想当演员，想当电影演员，当过推销员，在一家公司当过推销员
4. 大学教授，经济学教授，是一个大学教授，是一个大学的经济学教授
5. 有名的科学家，有名的企业家，很有名的运动员，特别有名的法国画家
6. 房地产经纪人，搞历史研究的学者，电视台的记者，最高法院的法官
7. 当过秘书，担任过经理助理，在一个学校当过保安，在一个公司做过实习生

U4-2.9 流利练习：描述工作经历（10分钟）

Fluency Drill: Listen to the entire passage once. Then listen again sentence by sentence. After each sentence, pause for three seconds, and then say the entire sentence aloud from memory. Repeat until you can say the sentence smoothly. Continue until you finish this paragraph.

以前老改行是搞教育的，在一个中学当体育老师。后来他不想当老师了，想改行做别的。有一个房地产公司正好需要一个推销员，所以老改行就去那里当推销员了。没过多久，他又觉得卖房子没意思，所以又开始找别的工作。后来几年里他又改过两次行，搞过进出口，做过秘书和经理助理。每个工作他都干不长就想找别的工作。这次他又到大新公司来找工作，他说当保安或者会计都可以，希望大新公司给他一个机会试一试。大新的人觉得他没有干过会计这一行，让他当会计可能不行。但是他看上去长得比较健壮，从前曾经当过体育老师，所以当保安应该还可以。大新的经理问他为什么老改行，他说，换一换不同的工作比较有意思，就像吃饭，天天吃一样的还会好吃吗？

U4-2.10 词语自测：行业与职业；身份与职务 （5分钟）

Vocabulary Self-Testing: Test yourself on the words and expressions in the following categories:

- 谈论行业职业
- 领域名称；行业名称
- 职业、身份
- 职务、身份

Suggestions:

1. **English-to-Chinese**: Use the English glossary of each section, covering the Chinese characters. Say each item aloud in Chinese as you read it in English. Mark the ones you fail to reproduce in Chinese for review (*you may also use flashcards*).

2. **Chinese-to-English:** Reverse the above to work on comprehension and character recognition. Mark the difficult characters for extra review.

3. **Memory Test**: Time yourself for three minutes and try to reproduce as many vocabulary items in the categories listed above as possible. You can type the items out in pinyin so that you don't lose count. When your time is up, go over the same sections in the vocabulary glossary to see what you have missed. Test yourself again to improve your performance.

第 三 课　　**爱好、专长、学历**
Lesson 3　　HOBBIES, SKILLS AND
　　　　　　EDUCATION

 U4-3.2　词句操练 Aural-Oral Drills

There are <u>six</u> drills in this lesson, which should be completed in two sessions (*A-D for Session 1, and E-F for Session 2, 20 min. each*). You need to complete each drill section twice to achieve intended results.

Important note: Before starting each drill, be sure to preview the glossary for an initial familiarization with the new words and expressions to be covered (*follow the glossary number as indicated in each drill*). For best results, also type the new words between or after the two rounds.

U4-3.2-A　兴趣爱好与专长 [词汇 U4.6]

说出名称

This section checks your familiarity with the vocabulary for **hobbies**, **interests**, and **specialties**. Give the equivalent of each item in Chinese as quickly as possible without consulting the glossary.

literature	history	foreign language	traveling
politics	technology	computer	socializing
reading	writing	music	outdoor activity
sports	art/drawing	dance	web design

U4-3.2-B　谈论兴趣爱好 [词汇 U4.6]

句式转换

This drill works on <u>three</u> common sentence forms for expressing one's **interests** and **hobbies**. Listen to the original sentence and the question. Then answer the question using one of these forms. In the second round, repeat the question before answering it.

> 最/特别爱好……; 对……最/特别感兴趣; (他)的兴趣爱好是……

例：王医生非常喜欢文学 (wénxué)。

回答问题：　王医生特别爱好什么？　　→　　王医生特别爱好文学。
　　　　　　王医生对什么特别感兴趣？　→　　王医生对文学特别感兴趣。

1. 张总经理最喜欢听音乐(yīnyuè)。
　　回答问题：张总经理对什么特别感兴趣？ →

2. 王主任特别喜欢体育(tǐyù)。
　　回答问题：王主任特别爱好什么？ →

3. 李律师一有空就打球、游泳(yóuyǒng)。
　　回答问题：李律师最爱好什么？ →

4. 刘秘书周末都在<u>阅读杂志</u>(yuèdúzázhì)。
   回答问题：刘秘书对什么特别感兴趣？　　　　　　　→

5. 那个小伙子对<u>历史</u>(lìshǐ) 最感兴趣。
   回答问题：那个小伙子的兴趣爱好是什么？　　　　　→

6. 那个女学生最爱好<u>舞蹈</u>(wǔdǎo)。
   回答问题：那个女学生的兴趣爱好是什么？　　　　　→

U4-3.2-C　特长专长：句式转换

This drill works on <u>two</u> common sentence forms for expressing one's **skills**. Listen to the original sentence and the question in each item. Then answer the question using one of the following forms. In the second round, repeat the question before answering it.

> 他的特长是……; 他在……方面有(一些)特长/很有特长

例：他哥哥的特长是<u>电脑</u>。

　　回答问题：他哥哥在什么方面有一些特长？　　　→　　　他在<u>电脑</u>方面很有特长。

1. 那位先生的特长是<u>人际沟通</u>。
   回答问题：那位先生在什么方面有一些特长？　　　→

2. 王小姐 在<u>社交</u>方面很有特长。
   回答问题：王小姐的特长是什么？　　　　　　　　→

3. 这位老师在<u>写作</u>方面有一些特长。
   回答问题：这位老师的特长是什么？　　　　　　　→

4. 这位女士的特长是<u>唱歌</u>。
   回答问题：这位女士在什么方面有特长？　　　　　→

U4-3.2-D　谈谈自己和身边的人：兴趣爱好和特长　　[词汇 U4.6]

First review the following sentence forms and expressions. Then answer the following questions as if you were being interviewed by a Chinese person. Be prepared to do an interview with your classmates.

> 兴趣爱好：我爱好……; 我对_____很(最、比较、非常、特别)有兴趣。
> 特长专长：我在_____方面有(一些)特长/专长; 我的特长/专长是……

1. 你有什么兴趣爱好？(请说三点)

2. 你有什么特长/专长？

3. 你的家人有哪些兴趣爱好和特长？

4. 你的朋友多半有哪方面的爱好和特长？(音乐、绘画、体育、电脑, 等等)

5. 你们国家的名牌大学比较看重学生的什么方面：能力、性格、兴趣爱好还是特长？

6. 你觉得找工作的时候什么比较重要？(能力、性格、兴趣爱好、特长/专长)

7. 你希望你的男朋友/女朋友有什么方面的爱好(和特长)？

8. 请你猜猜看你的中文老师有哪方面的爱好(和特长)。

U4-3.2-E 学历/教育背景 ［词汇 U4.7］

1. Read the following profile. Be prepared to answer questions based on the given information.

姓名：白云, 女, 23岁, 1.65米			
学校	北方大学商学院	年级	一年级硕士研究生
专业	旅游、饭店管理	兴趣爱好	阅读、绘画、舞蹈、体育
学位	文科学士	特长	绘画、外语
文凭	高中、大学	性格特点	外向、活泼、大方、合群
奖学金	3000元	工作经验	长城饭店经理助理, 实习生
证书	英语 6 级	将来发展	旅游业

2. Answer the following questions based on the above information.

1) 这个人叫什么名字? 是男性还是女性?

2) 这个人年龄有多大? 是什么个子? （有_____岁; 高/矮/中等个)

3) 他/她在哪个学校? 现在上几年级?

4) 他/她学什么专业?

5) 他/她现在有什么学位和文凭? 有什么证书?

6) 他/她现在有奖学金吗?

7) 他/她有什么方面的兴趣爱好和特长?

8) 他/她的性格怎么样? （是一个_____的人; 很/非常……）

9) 他/她有没有工作经验? （曾经在_____当过……）

10) 他/她打算将来搞什么? 在什么方面发展? （从事_____方面的工作)

U4-3.2-F 谈教育背景：相关动词 ［词汇 U4.8］

回答问题

The following drill focuses on the **verbs** commonly used to describe one's **educational background** in semi-formal or formal settings. Repeat this drill until you can easily recognize the phrases and answer the questions fluently. Familiarize yourself with the Chinese characters during the drills.

1. **就读** to study at

> 在学校就读; 就读于学校

回答问题：你现在在哪个学校就读?

你以前曾经在哪个学校就读过?

2. **获得**　to receive (award, certificate etc.)

> 获得奖学金、学位、证书

回答问题：你<u>获得</u>过什么：<u>奖学金</u>、<u>学位</u>、<u>证书</u>?

　　　　　　你什么时候<u>获得</u>过学位/会<u>获得</u>学位? 是什么学位?

3. **组织**　to organize; organization

> 组织活动; 一个组织

回答问题：你<u>组织</u>过什么课外活动?

　　　　　　你参加过学校的什么<u>组织</u>吗? 是什么方面的<u>组织</u>?

4. **培训**　to train; training

> 培训雇员; 受哪方面的培训; 受过多长时间的培训

回答问题：你在哪些学校<u>受过</u>中文<u>培训</u>? 你<u>受过</u>多久的中文<u>培训</u>? 几个月? 几年?

　　　　　　除了中文以外，你还<u>受过</u>什么方面的<u>培训</u>?

流利强化　Fluency Enhancement

 U4-3.8　语块练习：性格、兴趣爱好和特长 [词汇 U4.5-4.7]

Chunking Exercise: Listen to and repeat each phrase aloud. Then type it with 100% accuracy. Also write all phrases by hand.

---

1. 不够活泼开朗，看上去比较严肃，说起话来不够热情，给人的感觉是|很冷漠

2. 是一个很风趣的人，说起话来很幽默，给人的印象是|非常有教养

3. 比较爱好上网，对体育最感兴趣，特别喜欢阅读和听音乐

4. 兴趣爱好很广，特别爱好文学和艺术，非常爱好户外运动

5. 不爱好音乐，对网络和网页设计|不感兴趣，对科技方面的东西|不太感兴趣

6. 在外语方面有一些特长，特长是在外语方面，在音乐方面|也很有专长

7. 给人的感觉是|对政治没有兴趣，给人的印象是|在写作方面很有特长

8. 获得硕士学位，获得奖学金，获得实习机会，受过专业培训

U4-3.9 流利练习：描述印象 （10分钟）
Fluency Drill: Listen to the following sentences. After each sentence, pause for two to three seconds, and then repeat the whole sentence aloud from memory. You should repeat each item until you can say the entire sentence smoothly and accurately with the correct tones.

1. 他是一个(性格)很外向的人，非常活泼开朗，也很合群。

2. 她给人的印象是|比较文静、有点腼腆，但有时|她也非常活泼。

3. 他比较爱好户外运动，比如说，爬山、滑雪、打球，等等。

4. 她在外语方面|有一些特长，会(说)三种外语，而且阅读能力|也很不错。

5. 他特别爱好文学和艺术，也很喜欢旅游，但对电脑网络等|科技方面的东西|不感兴趣。

6. 她的特长是在科技方面，对网络和网页设计|非常感兴趣。

7. 别看他看上去比较严肃，有时给人一种|不够热情的感觉，其实|他是一个很风趣的人，说起话来非常幽默。

8. 他兴趣爱好很广，体育、文学、音乐、电脑等|他都喜欢，特别是在音乐方面|很有专长。

U4-3.10 个人概况：介绍学校和专业
Introduce your school and field of study.

1) 你向一个中国学生介绍自己的大学：有什么学院、多少系、什么系，可以学什么（文科、理科、工科、商科等）；什么时候应该决定自己的专业或主修；修什么课、哪些课程有意思；另外，校园生活是怎么样的，课外活动、参加社团等。

2) 介绍自己的专业：向同学介绍自己的学院和主修，说明自己为什么选这个学院或者专业，学位有哪些课程要求，学分要求，必修课，选修课等，毕业以后有哪些机会。

U4-3.11 写作练习：描述人物印象 (10分钟)
Describe two students you recently met at school: their **looks**, **character traits**, and **interests**.
Discuss your impression of them.

U4-3.12 词语自测：爱好、专长、学历 (5–10分钟)
Test yourself for <u>five</u> minutes and see how many words and expressions you can reproduce from memory in the categories below. Type them out. When your time is up, go over the same sections in the glossary to see what you have missed.

• 兴趣爱好、特长专长   • 教育背景

U4-4.2 词句操练 Aural-Oral Drills

There are **two** drills in this lesson, which can be completed in one session (*15 min.*). You need to complete each drill twice to achieve intended results.

U4-4.2-A 谈日常工作和工作经验：动词名词搭配 [词汇 U4.9-4.10]

This drill works on *verbs* commonly used to describe general **tasks and routines** in a work setting. Repeat this drill until you can easily recognize the phrases and answer the questions fluently. Familiarize yourself with the Chinese characters during the drills. Make an effort to memorize the **verb-noun** collocations.

1. 处理：处理事情、事务、资料、文件

回答问题：你每天都有很多事情要处理吗？是私事(自己的事情)还是公事？
在办公室当秘书或者助理，需要处理什么事务？(日常事务、资料文件)

2. 管理：管理事务；对人或事的管理

Note: "管理" can be used as a *verb* or a *noun*.

回答问题：你做过什么方面的管理工作？(管理学生、学生事务)
你认为这个学校对学生事务的管理怎么样？

3. 协助：协助人做一件事；需要别人的协助

Note: "协助" can be used as a *verb* or a *noun*.

回答问题：有些学生协助教授做研究。你有没有机会协助你的老师做什么？
在工作实习的时候，你协助别人做什么？(处理资料文件、处理日常事务)
在学习和工作的时候，你需要不需要别人的协助？

4. 具有：具有能力、经验、知识

Note: "具有" **cannot** be followed by a *monosyllabic* and *concrete noun*.

回答问题：你具有什么方面的能力？(如：组织能力、学习外语的能力)
你具有什么方面的专业知识？(如：外语知识、电脑知识)

5. 负责：负责X方面的事务；是负责人

回答问题：你负责过什么方面的事务？你们学校学生组织的负责人是谁？
如果我们明天开一个晚会，你想负责什么？(如：买食品、布置房间等)

6. 积累：积累经验、知识、词汇

回答问题：近几年来，你积累了什么方面的经验？(如：工作经验、学习经验)
这个学期以来，你积累了多少中文词汇？(500？800？1000？)

U4-4.2-B 口语转为书面语 [词汇 U4.9-4.10]

This drill works on the conversion from the **colloquial** to the **formal** style. Repeat the sentence in the colloquial style, and then rephrase it in the formal style by following the hint provided.

例：他以前在北京大学上学。　（曾在……就读）　　→　　他以前曾在北京大学就读。

1. 上大学的时候他得过奖学金。(大学期间, 曾获得……)　→
2. 两年前他拿到了硕士学位。　(获得)　　　　　　　　→
3. 他很有经验, 也很有知识。　(具有丰富的……)　　　→
4. 他学过三年的中文。　　　　(曾受过……培训)　　　→
5. 他管办公室的事情。　　　　（负责, 处理, 事务）　　→
6. 今年她是这个项目的负责人。(担任, 主管)　　　　　→
7. 他帮经理做一些日常事务。　(协助, 处理)　　　　　→
8. 她帮主管做过几个项目。　　(曾协助, 完成)　　　　→
9. 去年他在一家大公司工作过。(曾受雇于……)　　　　→
10. 她很会跟人交往、沟通。　　(具有很强的＿＿＿能力)　→

流利强化Fluency Enhancement

U4-4.9 语块练习：能力和经验 [词汇 U4.9-4.11]

Chunking Exercise: The following phrases are commonly used for talking about one's **education** and **work experience**. Try to memorize the *verb-noun* collocations. Repeat each phrase aloud a few times and type it as you say it. Then write all phrases by hand.

1. 具有丰富经验,　　具有沟通能力,　　具有外语能力,　　具有管理经验
   jùyǒu fēngfùjīngyàn　　jùyǒu gōutōngnénglì　　jùyǒu wàiyúnénglì　　jùyǒu guǎnlǐjīngyàn

2. 组织课外活动,　　负责日常事务,　　管理学生事务,　　管理资料档案
   zǔzhī kèwàihuódòng　　fùzé rìchángshìwù　　guǎnlǐ xuéshēngshìwù　　guǎnlǐ zīliàodàng'àn

3. 处理文件资料,　　协助处理日常事务,　　完成项目计划,　　完成工作报告
   chǔlǐ wénjiànzīliào　　xiézhù chǔlǐ rìchángshìwù　　wánchéng xiàngmùjìhuà　　wánchéng gōngzuòbàogào

4. 积累了很多专业知识,　　积累了丰富的工作经验
   jīlěile hěnduō zhuānyèzhīshi　　jīlěile fēngfùde gōngzuòjīngyàn

U4-4.10 填写个人简况表 (15分钟)

1. 熟悉常用词组

These are stock phrases for one's **résumé** and **personal information**. Note that these four-character set phrases are commonly used and each should be memorized as a chunk. Read each phrase aloud twice and type it out as you say it each time. Type each phrase as one unit and do not insert space between the pinyin syllables.

个人简历	本人概况	教育背景	工作经历/经验	联系电话/地址
gèrénjiǎnlì	běnréngàikuàng	jiàoyùbèijǐng	gōngzuòjīnglì/jīngyàn	liánxìdiànhuà/dìzhǐ

电子信箱	毕业院校	所学课程	业余爱好	本人性格	特别技能
diànzǐxìnxiāng	bìyèyuànxiào	suǒxuékèchéng	yèyú'àihào	běnrénxìnggé	tèbiéjìnéng

第四单元 · 介绍人物简况

2. 填写个人简况表

Read the following form for comprehension. Then create a profile of a person (real or imagined) by filling in his/her personal particulars.

个人概况		工作经历/经验	
姓名		单位/公司	
年龄		职务	
性别		工作经历 1	
职业、身份			
联系电话		工作经历 2	
电子信箱			
教育背景		其　他	
所在/毕业院校		性格特点	
专业/主修		兴趣爱好	
毕业时间		专长/特别技能	
学位文凭/证书		将来发展方向	

U4-4.11 流利练习：描述面试经历 (5分钟)

Fluency Drill: Use the following paragraph in the story "我的面试经历" for a fluency drill. Listen to one complete sentence, pause for two or more seconds, and then say the whole sentence aloud <u>from memory</u>. Repeat the sentence until you can say it smoothly with the correct tones. Continue until you finish the paragraph.

> 　　我在床上躺了一天，想来想去，觉得还是不能放弃，还是再去试一次吧。两天后，我找到公司的营销部。营销部的钱经理正在做工作计划，他冷冰冰地对我说，今天助理不在，很多事务得他自己处理，很忙，让我去人事部找王经理。我只好再去人事部，没想到秘书告诉我，王经理不在，要我一周以后再来。我一听心都凉了：我来了四次了，一次比一次不顺利，一周以后再来不知又有什么新情况？我感到非常失望，不知该怎么办。

U4-4.12 词语自测：工作经验 (5分钟)

Test yourself for <u>three</u> minutes and see how many items from the following categories you can reproduce. Type them out for easy counting. Then check the glossary to see what you have missed.

- 工作经验：相关名词
- 工作经验：相关动词

第 五 课 | **介绍人物简况**
Lesson 5 | INTRODUCING A PERSON'S PROFILE

 U4-5.1 语段示例：自我介绍

Read Examples 1-3 in Lesson 5 in the Textbook closely and note the punctuation marks, as well as sentence connections and topic transitions.

U4-5.2 语段练习：介绍他人

Use the paragraph template in Examples 4 and 5 in this lesson to complete the following writing exercises.

1. 介绍一个朋友
2. 介绍/推荐一个人

单元测试与报告 Unit Assignments

For the unit review and assignments, please consult Appendices 1-3 for a guide on language use, grammar, and discourse structure.

U4-5.3 词语测试：本单元词语句式及语言结构

Vocabulary Test: Review the words and expressions in this unit and get ready for a test.

U4-5.4 语段写作：自我介绍

Writing: Write a detailed **self-introduction** including the following information. Read the writing examples in this lesson as a guide.

• 个人信息 (姓名、年龄等个人情况)
• 教育背景
• 性格爱好、特长/专长
• 工作经验

活动程序和要求 Guidelines and Instructions for the Tasks

1. 阅读讨论活动要求 Guidelines for the Reading and Discussion Activities

Your good preparation for and active participation in the class discussions are required. Follow the instructions below (unless otherwise specified by your instructor).

For reading texts: You are expected to read each text in advance as you need to answer comprehension questions and share views in class. Use a notebook or flashcards to collect useful words and expressions from the reading texts.

For your assigned task: If you have been assigned to lead a class discussion activity (by yourself or your group), you (or your group) should also prepare your activity by following these guidelines:

1) Your activity should last about <u>five</u> minutes.

2) Keep your activity steps simple, clear, and efficient; do not try to accomplish too many things!

3) Limit your new vocabulary terms, if any, to five. Write the new terms on the blackboard to facilitate comprehension.

4) Have your outline, procedure, or script checked by your teacher in advance.

2. 模拟任务说明 Instructions for the Simulation Tasks

These simulations can be done as a class activity in groups of 3 or 4, or as an oral exam with the teacher. You should prepare for the tasks by reviewing vocabulary and sentence structures, as well as examples of paragraph level presentation.
Use the following scenarios to prepare for the tasks for the class activity.

模拟任务1：工作面试 (A Job Interview)

_____办公室/公司想找一个人做_____工作，有1个申请人来参加工作面试。面试官（1或2人）问申请人一些问题，并请申请人介绍自己的工作经验和学历。申请人也要说明为什么觉得自己是一个合适的人选。面试以后，两个面试官表达自己对申请人的印象和看法，说明为什么合适/不合适。（工作面试4-5分钟；表达看法2分钟）

模拟任务2：介绍朋友 (Helping a Lonely Person find a Partner)

你们两个人在一个交友介绍所（Dating Agency）工作。有人请你们为他/她（们）介绍朋友。你们要先和这X个人面谈，了解他/她（们）的学历、工作经验以及兴趣爱好特长等背景情况，以及他/她（们）的要求。然后你们讨论应该给他/她（们）介绍什么样的人。你们两个人应该分别做一个推荐，并说明为什么。（面谈每个人4分钟；做推荐每个人2分钟）

3. 定时写作 Timed Composition (20 分钟)

Choose one of the following topics and complete this task within 20 minutes using the typing method. Your writing should be at least two paragraphs in length, with general statements, supporting details, and examples. Try to include the following information as you see fit to make your descriptions substantial.

生理特征、穿着打扮、言谈举止、性格特点、兴趣爱好、特长、教育背景、工作经验

a. 推荐一个人

你的学生会里需要一个委员组织各种活动。有几个会员已经自愿报名担任这个职务。你发现你的同学中有一个人（也是会员）是一个更合适的人选。于是你写一个邮件给学生会会长和副会长推荐这个人。你得介绍这个人的个人背景和经验，并说明为什么他/她是最合适的人选。

Your student association needs someone to coordinate association activities. Several members have already volunteered for the job. However, you find that one of your classmates (also a member of the association) is a stronger candidate. You therefore write an email to the association president and vice president to make a recommendation. Provide the person's profile and explain why you believe he/she is the best fit for the job.

b. 为朋友介绍语伴

你为一个中国朋友介绍一个可互相学习语言的语伴。这个中国朋友比较腼腆，26岁，比较喜欢待在室内，爱好阅读、音乐，以及上网。你有两个很好的朋友可能是合适的语伴。你给中国朋友写一封邮件，介绍这两个朋友，并比较他们的不同特点。

You are trying to find a language partner for your Chinese friend. Your Chinese friend is a shy person, 26, likes to stay indoors, and loves reading, music and Internet surfing. You have two close friends who might be suitable. Write an email to your Chinese friend and introduce and compare these two people.

c. 谈论一个新朋友

你最近交的一个中国朋友想跟你约会。虽然你很喜欢这个人，可也有一些方面不太满意。你不知道应不应该去，所以想问问另一个中国朋友。写一个邮件，详细描述你的新朋友各方面的情况，包括你喜欢的和不喜欢的，问这位中国朋友有什么建议。

A new Chinese friend you recently met would like to go on a date with you. You like this person in general, but there are some things about him/her that you are not completely pleased with. You are unsure whether you should see him/her and decide to ask another Chinese friend of yours for advice. Write an email for advice and give detailed descriptions of this new person, and what you like and dislike about him/her.

第五单元	谈论自然现象	第 一 课	自然现象
UNIT **5**	TALKING ABOUT NATURE	Lesson 1	NATURE AND WEATHER

 U5-1.2 词句操练 Aural-Oral Drills

There are <u>four</u> drills in this lesson, which can be completed in one session (*20 min.*). You need to complete each drill twice to achieve intended results.

Important note: Before starting each drill, be sure to preview the glossary for an initial familiarization with the new words and expressions to be covered (*follow the glossary number as indicated in each drill*). For best results, also type the new words between or after the two rounds.

U5-1.2-A 谈论天气情况 ［词汇 U5.0-5.1］
看图回答问题
This drill focuses on the "有-structure" for **describing weather conditions** or **giving a forecast**. Listen to the questions carefully and then answer each question based on the picture(s). In the second round, repeat each question aloud before answering it, looking at the characters.

用"有"表达天气状况
Note: "有" is mostly used for future events (e.g., will rain/snow) or an existing condition (e.g., was/is/will be foggy/icy).

1. 今天有太阳吗？有云吗？云多不多？是白云还是乌云 (wūyún / dark clouds)？

2. 这几天有雨吗？是什么雨：小雨、大雨、阵雨还是暴雨？

3. 这个地方什么时候常常有雷阵雨？夏天还是秋天？

4. 明天会不会有雪？是小雪、大雪，还是暴风雪？

5. 今天开车安全吗？有大雾、路上有雪、有冰、有霜？

U5-1.2-B 谈论天气情况：动词用法 ［词汇 U5.1］
根据提示回答问题
This drill works on common **verbs** associated with **weather** and **natural phenomenon**. Repeat the verb and the corresponding sentence. Then listen to the question(s) and answer it/them based on the given information. In the second round, repeat each question before answering it.

下雨	下雪	刮风	结冰	打雷	闪电	上升	下降	晴	阴	转
xiàyǔ	xiàxuě	guāfēng	jiébīng	dǎléi	shǎndiàn	shàngshēng	xiàjiàng	qíng	yīn	zhuǎn

1. **下雨**：今天下了两场雨，现在雨停了。
   回答问题：今天下雨了吗？下了几场雨？雨下得大不大？雨停了吗？

2. **下雪**：明天要下一天(的)小雪。
   回答问题：明天有雪吗？雪大不大？明天的雪会下多久？

3. **刮风**：今天刮了一天大风，现在风停了。
   回答问题：风刮得大不大？风停了没有？

4. **结冰**：地上的水结冰了。
   回答问题：路上结冰了，你今天还要开车吗？

5. **打雷、闪电**：刚才<u>打雷</u>、<u>闪电</u>。
   回答问题：刚才又打雷又闪电，我看马上就要下大雨了，你还出去运动吗？

6. **上升/下降**：气温<u>下降</u>了10度，<u>降到</u>零下5度。
   回答问题：今天的天气怎么样？气温是多少？

7. **晴、阴**：今天早<u>上是阴天</u>；今天下午<u>天晴了</u>；明天会是<u>晴天</u>。
   回答问题：今天是阴天还是晴天？明天会不会下雨？

8. **转**：<u>阴转晴</u>；<u>北风转南风</u>
   回答问题：今天天气怎么样？还是阴天吗？是什么风？

U5-1.2-C 词语复习："变"的用法

This section reviews the usage of **"变"** with the topic of weather. Read the different "变-" forms, and then repeat each sentence as you hear it, noting the appropriate "变-" form used in each restatement. In the second round, restate the initial sentences without looking at the text.

> 变化   多变   变了   会变   变____了   变得……   A变成B

1. 这几天天气变化很大。 → 这几天天气很<u>多变</u>。
2. 今天和昨天的天气不一样。 → 今天的天气<u>变了</u>。
3. 昨天很热，今天有点冷。 → 今天天气<u>变</u>冷了。
4. 昨天是晴天，今天是阴天。 → 昨天是晴天，今天<u>变成</u>阴天了。
5. 这几天一天比一天热。 → 这几天天气<u>变得</u>越来越热了。
6. 云越来越黑，下午可能是阴天。 → 云<u>变</u>黑了，天可能会<u>变阴</u>。
7. 明天天气可能和今天不一样。 → 明天天气可能<u>会变</u>。

U5-1.2-D 回答问题：谈谈这里的天气 [词汇 U5.2-5.3]

This section reviews basic words and expressions for talking about **weather** in daily conversations. Answer the question(s) as quickly as possible. In the second round, repeat each question as if you were getting information from someone.

1. 你现在住的地区夏季热吗？<u>最高气温</u>是多少？是华氏度还是摄氏度？
2. 冬天<u>最低气温</u>会不会到零下？哪个月最冷？
3. 这里什么时候是<u>雨季</u>？雨季的时候下多少天的雨？是大雨还是小雨？
4. 这几天你们这里的天气<u>情况</u>怎么样？是晴天、阴天、雨天，还是多云天气？
5. 今天白天<u>出</u>太阳了吗？是蓝天白云还是灰色的<u>天空</u>？
6. 昨天晚上晴还是阴？<u>天空</u>上看得到星星吗？
7. 今天的<u>气温</u>情况怎么样？跟昨天比起来是<u>上升</u>了还是<u>下降</u>了？
8. 今天的气温比昨天<u>上升/下降</u>了多少度？<u>升到/降到</u>多少度了？
9. 今天<u>有没有</u>风？你觉得是南风还是北风？风大不大？
10. 今年下过大雨或暴雨吗？是在什么<u>季节</u>？下过几场？
11. 这个冬天你们这个地方下过<u>几场</u>雪？有没有下过暴风雪？
12. 冬天的时候这里路上会不会<u>结冰</u>？如果下大雪、结冰，你会怎么去上学/上班？

13. 在你们这里，<u>冬季</u>有多冷？需要什么样的穿着？

14. 如果让你<u>选择</u>，你最喜欢什么样的<u>气候</u>？（如：南方还是北方、热还是冷？）

15. 如果你找工作，会不会因为天气的原因而不选择一些地方？（如：喜欢那个工作，但不喜欢那里的气候，所以就不去）

流利强化 Fluency Enhancement

U5-1.9　语块练习：描述自然现象和天气状况 [词汇 U5.0-5.3]

Chunking Exercise: Listen to and read each phrase aloud, and then type it out with 100% accuracy. For best results, also select some phrases to write by hand.

---

1. 下雨、下小雨、下暴雨、下阵雨，今天下了两场大雨，现在雨停了
2. 下雪、下大雪、下暴风雪，去年下过几场雪，雪下得很大，明天要下一天的雪
3. 刮风、刮大风，风刮得很大，今天刮了一天大风，现在风停了
4. 结冰，结了很厚的冰，地上的水结成冰了，路上结冰了，冰还没有化
5. 打雷、闪电，刚才打雷打得很大，雷声很大，刚才又打雷又闪电
6. 上升/下降，气温上升了，上升了5度，气温下降了，降到零下5度了
7. 天气情况，天气变化，自然现象，天气预报，30摄氏度，80华氏度
8. **晴、阴**：今天早上是阴天，今天下午天晴了，明天会晴还是会阴？
9. **转**：阴转晴、晴转阴，风向转了，北风转成南风了，雨转成雪了
10. **变**：天气很多变，气温变化很大，天变了，天变冷了，天变得越来越冷

U5-1.10　速读/巩固：《盘古开天地》（5分钟）

Speed Reading/Review: Follow the steps below.

1. Read the story in Lesson 1 within three minutes focusing on meaning. You are expected to get the main ideas and recognize the core vocabulary we have covered.
2. Without looking at the book, try to recall the vocabulary items in the passage related to nature and universe.
3. Read or listen to the entire passage one more time, focusing on sentence connections and transitions this time.

U5-1.11　流利练习：描述自然现象—名词（5分钟）

Fluency Drill: Listen to the <u>third</u> paragraph of the story "盘古开天地" sentence by sentence. If you need to work on a character reading rather than the pronunciation and tones, you can also read along. After you hear or read each sentence, pause for <u>three</u> seconds, and then read the whole sentence aloud <u>from memory</u>. You should repeat each sentence until you can say it smoothly and accurately. Continue to finish the paragraph.

就这样过了一万八千年，这时天与地离得很远很远了，盘古也累得倒下了。这时他的声音变成了雷，呼出的气变成了风，左眼变成太阳，右眼变成月亮，身体变成了高山和田地，血液变成了江河，汗毛变成了花草树木，骨头和牙齿变成了金属和石头，头发和胡子变成了星星……

第一课·自然现象

第 二 课 | **自然灾害**
Lesson 2 | NATURAL DISASTERS

 U5-2.2 词句操练 Aural-Oral Drills

There are **five** drills in this lesson, which can be completed in two sessions (*A-C for Session 1, 15 min.; D-E for Session 2, 10 min.*). You need to complete each section twice to achieve intended results.

Important note: Before starting each drill, be sure to preview the glossary for an initial familiarization with the new words and expressions to be covered (*follow the glossary number as indicated in each drill*). For best results, also type the new words between or after the two rounds.

U5-2.2-A 描述灾情 [词汇 U5.4-5.6]

看图回答问题

This section works on the basic verbs to describe common disasters. First review the following key *verbs*. Repeat each *verb* and examples and **note** the form in each case. In the second round, read the Chinese characters aloud with improved fluency.

发生	遭受	袭击	垮/倒塌	冲	淹	刮	压	砸
fāshēng	zāoshòu	xíjī	kuǎ / dǎotā	chōng	yān	guā	yā	zá

1. **发生**：发生了旱灾；发生过水灾、会发生洪灾

2. **遭受/遭到袭击**：遭受/到台风（龙卷风、洪水、暴雨）的袭击

3. **垮/倒塌**：地震使房屋倒塌；房屋被震垮/震塌

4. **冲**：洪水冲垮房屋、冲走人/冲走财产；房屋被冲垮、冲塌

5. **淹**：洪水淹了房屋街道；房屋遭到水淹；人被淹死

6. **刮**：刮倒/断了树；树被风刮倒/断；风刮走了屋顶；屋顶被刮走；刮得沙尘满天飞

7. **压**：树被压断；房屋被压垮/塌；车被压坏

8. **砸**：重物砸下来；砸伤/死了人；人被砸伤砸死

U5-2.2-B 谈论地震 [词汇 U5.5-5.6]

根据提示回答问题

This section works on basic terms for earthquakes. Review the key terms first. Then for each drill item, listen to the question carefully and answer it accordingly. In the second round, read the questions aloud and answer them again with improved fluency.

震塌	震垮	伤亡	受伤	死亡	交通	困难	采取	措施	疏散
zhèntā	zhènkuǎ	shāngwáng	shòushāng	sǐwáng	jiāotōng	kùnnán	cǎiqǔ	cuòshī	shūsàn

1. 昨晚这个地区发生了什么灾害：洪水、地震还是龙卷风？

2. 房屋情况怎么样：被震塌、震垮、压垮还是被冲垮？

3. 伤亡情况怎么样？（如：伤亡不太大；很多人受伤、少数人死亡）

4. 交通情况怎么样？是不是很困难、很不方便，还是不受影响？

5. 应该采取什么措施？发布警报、疏散到安全地带，还是待在房子里？

U5-2.2-C 谈论洪灾 [词汇 U5.5-5.6]

根据提示回答问题

This section works on basic terms for **flood**. Review the key terms first. Listen to the question(s) carefully and answer it accordingly. In the second round, read the questions aloud and answer them again with improved fluency.

淹	淹水	淹没	淹死	积水	冲垮	冲走	倒塌	失踪	疏散
yān	yānshuǐ	yānmò	yānsǐ	jīshuǐ	chōngkuǎ	chōngzǒu	dǎotā	shīzōng	shūsàn

1. 昨天这个地区发生了什么灾害：洪灾、旱灾，还是台风？
2. 房屋情况怎么样：遭到水淹、被洪水淹没，还是已经倒塌？
3. 路面交通情况怎么样：有积水、积水很深，交通不便，还是不受影响？
4. 灾民情况怎么样：被大水冲走、很多人失踪，还是被淹死？
5. 应该采取什么措施：疏散到安全地带、发布警报，还是马上救援、救助灾区？

U5-2.2-D 谈论台风 [词汇 U5.5-5.6]

根据提示回答问题

This section works on basic terms for hurricane or typhoon. Review the key terms first. Listen to the question carefully and answer it according to the hints provided. In the second round, read the questions aloud and answer them again with improved fluency.

遭受袭击	造成影响	停电/水	刮掉	刮断	压垮	受伤	死亡
zāoshòu xíjī	zàochéng yǐngxiǎng	tíngdiàn / shuǐ	guādiào	guāduàn	yākuǎ	shòushāng	sǐwáng

1. 今早这个地区发生了什么灾害？遭到什么的袭击？（台风）
2. 台风造成了什么影响？（10万户人家停电/停水；交通不便）
3. 房屋情况怎么样？（一些房屋的屋顶被刮掉；有的大树被刮断，把房子压垮。）
4. 路面情况怎么样？（台风造成交通困难/不便。）
5. 伤亡情况怎么样？（有少数人受伤，但没有人死亡。）
6. 采取了什么措施？（发布了台风警报，正在帮助灾民疏散到安全地带。）

U5-2.2-E 谈谈自己的国家

Round 1: Imagine you are chatting with a Chinese teacher or friend, and answer the following questions.

Round 2: Read each question aloud for character recognition and answer it again with improved fluency.

1. 在你们国家，最常发生的灾害是什么？
2. 最近一次灾害是什么？什么时候、在哪里发生的？
3. 那次灾害造成了什么问题？
4. 灾害发生的时候，哪些地区受到影响？（如：房屋、交通、水电等）
5. 你现在住的这个地区会受什么灾害的袭击：台风、飓风、龙卷风、暴风雪？
6. 如果现在这个地方发生地震或者水灾，你觉得政府应该采取什么措施？
7. 如果你不马上疏散或离开，会发生什么事情？

U5-2.2-F 听力练习：天气预报

(This activity can be done in class or as a follow-up assignment.)

1. Listen to the two short passages (weather forecast and advice for severe weather) without looking at the script. Try to figure out the meaning of the unfamiliar words from the context.
2. Without looking at the script, recall the descriptions from the listening clip and jot them down.
3. Answer the comprehension questions below based on your notes.
4. Compare your notes against the scripts that follow the questions.

1) **天气预报**

   问题：a. 今天白天是什么天气？　　b. 夜间天气有什么变化？

   　　　c. 明后天有什么天气情况？　　d. 可能会发生什么问题？

2) **预警/警报**

   　　　a. 警报说明天天气会有什么情况？ _____

   　　　b. 这个天气情况是什么造成的？ _____

   　　　c. 哪些地区将会受到影响？ _____

   　　　d. 需要注意什么问题？ _____

（一）天气预报

今天白天，阴，最高气温23摄氏度。今天夜间，由于受附近地区台风影响，将有大风，最低气温16摄氏度。明后两天有50到70毫米暴雨，风力7至8级，气温也将下降3至5摄氏度。请大家做好防洪准备。

（二）中央气象台8日上午发布暴雨和海上大风警报

受第9号热带风暴"麦莎"的影响，预计今天中午到明天中午，山东大部、河北东部、北京市、天津市等地区将有大到暴雨。同时，黄海和东海北部沿海地区将有9-10级大风。请有关单位注意防范暴雨带来的洪水、泥石流、山体滑坡等灾害。

—据中央气象台发布的警报缩写

流利强化 Fluency Enhancement

U5-2.8 语块练习：描述灾害 [词汇 U5.4-5.6]

Chunking Exercise: Read each set aloud, and then type it with 100% output accuracy. Also select some phrases to write by hand.

1. 发生， 发生了地震， 那里发生了特大水灾， 去年这里发生过旱灾
   fāshēng　fāshēngle dìzhèn　nàli fāshēngle tèdàshuǐzāi　qùnián zhèli fāshēngguò hànzāi

2. 遭到袭击， 受到袭击， 遭受到台风袭击， 昨天那里遭到龙卷风袭击
   zāodàoxíjī　shòudàoxíjī　zāoshòudào táifēng xíjī　zuótiān nàli zāodào lóngjuǎnfēng xíjī

3. 受影响， 受天气影响， 受到很大影响， 洪水使交通受到很大影响
   shòuyǐngxiǎng　shòutiānqì yǐngxiǎng　shòudào hěndà yǐngxiǎng　hóngshuǐ shǐ jiāotōng shòudào hěndà yǐngxiǎng

4. 垮/倒塌， 地震使房屋倒塌， 房屋被震垮震塌
   kuǎ / dǎotā　dìzhèn shǐ fángwū dǎotā　fángwū bèi zhènkuǎzhèntā

5. 冲： 洪水冲垮了房屋， 人被洪水冲走， 房屋被冲垮冲塌
   chōng　hóngshuǐ chōngkuǎle fángwū　rén bèihóngshuǐ chōngzǒu　fángwū bèi chōngkuǎchōngtā

6. 淹： 洪水淹了房屋和街道， 房屋遭到水淹， 水淹进房子里， 人被淹死
   yān　hóngshuǐ yānle fángwū hé jiēdào　fángwū zāodào shuǐyān　shuǐ yānjìn fángzili　rén bèiyānsǐ

7. 刮： 风刮倒了大树， 树被风刮断， 屋顶被风刮走， 东西被刮得满天飞
   guā　fēng guādǎole dàshù　shù bèifēngguāduàn　wūdǐng bèifēngguāzǒu　dōngxi bèiguāde mǎntiānfēi

8. 压： 树被压断， 房屋被压垮/塌， 车被压扁压坏
   yā　shù bèiyāduàn　fángwū bèiyākuǎ/tā　chē bèiyābiǎn yāhuài

9. 砸： 重物砸下来， 砸伤/死了人， 人被砸伤砸死
   zá　zhòngwù záxiàlai　záshāng/sǐle rén　rén bèizáshāngzásǐ

10. 采取措施， 采取救援措施， 离开危险地带， 把灾民疏散到安全地带
    cǎiqǔcuòshī　cǎiqǔ jiùyuáncuòshī　líkāi wēixiǎndìdài　bǎzāimín shūsàndào ānquándìdài

11. 灾害情况/灾情， 伤亡情况， 路面交通情况， 救灾情况
    zāihàiqíngkuàng/zāiqíng　shāngwángqíngkuàng　lùmiàn jiāotōngqíngkuàng　jiùzāiqíngkuàng

12. 造成， 带来， 造成停电停水， 带来很大不便， 造成很多人失踪
    zàochéng　dàilái　zàochéng tíngdiàn tíngshuǐ　dàilái hěndàbúbiàn　zàochéng hěnduōrén shīzōng

U5-2.9 速读/巩固：《谈谈台风》（5分钟）

Speed Reading/Review: Follow the steps below.

1. Read the text section by section, focusing on meaning. Complete reading each section within one minute.
2. Without looking at the passage, try to answer the questions in each part.
3. Read the entire passage again, noting the sentence connections and transitions.

U5-2.10 流利练习：描述灾害（5分钟）

Fluency Drill: Work on the following section from the reading passage "谈谈台风". Listen to it sentence by sentence. After each sentence, pause for three seconds, and then say the whole sentence aloud from memory. Repeat a sentence until you can say it smoothly and accurately.

> 　　台风会带来严重的危害。有一次台风袭击了中国的浙江省，使附近的安徽省和上海市也受到影响。一天之内，浙江省的受灾人口有840万，倒塌的房屋有13000多间，造成的直接经济损失高达65.5亿。同时，由于受台风影响，上海连续下了6小时的暴雨，造成上海的80多条街道淹水，也影响了地铁的运行。

U5-2.11 写作练习：描述一次灾害（10分钟）

Writing Exercise: Describe a natural disaster you know or have read about. Provide as many details as you can. When you are done, be sure to check your Chinese characters for typing errors. Follow one of the sentence structures to begin your description:

> XX年XX月XX日，在X国的X发生了地震/旱灾/火灾
>
> XX年XX月XX日，X国的X地区遭到台风/暴雨的袭击

U5-2.12 词语自测：自然现象、自然灾害（5分钟）

Vocabulary Self-Testing: Test yourself on the vocabulary items of the following topics. Use the **English-to-Chinese** translation (or vice versa) method, or the timed memory test.

- Nature and the universe
- Weather conditions and forecast
- Verbs for everyday weather and natural phenomenon (to rain, snow, freeze...)
- Terms associated with major disasters such as earthquakes, floods, hurricanes or tornados
- *Verb-noun* collocations with "造成" and "带来".

第 三 课　气候与感觉
Lesson 3　CLIMATE AND
PERSONAL FEELINGS

 U5-3.2　词句操练 Aural-Oral Drills

There are <u>four</u> drills in this lesson, which should be completed in one session (*30 min.*). You need to complete each drill twice to achieve intended results.

Important note: Before starting each drill, be sure to preview the glossary for an initial familiarization with the new words and expressions to be covered (*follow the glossary number as indicated in each drill*). For best results, also type the new words between or after the two rounds.

U5-3.2-A　天气/气候特点　[词汇 U5.7]

This section focuses on common terms used to describe characteristics of climate. First read the following terms aloud with comprehension. Then answer the general questions.

季节	潮湿	干燥	暖和	寒冷	炎热	凉快	雨季	多风
jìjié	cháoshī	gānzào	nuǎnhuo	hánlěng	yánrè	liángkuai	yǔjì	duōfēng
湿度	温度	气温	四季分明		四季如春/如夏/如冬			
shīdù	wēndù	qìwēn	sìjìfēnmíng		sìjìrúchūn / rúxià / rúdōng			

1. 一般来说，哪个季节比较<u>潮湿</u>？是不是因为<u>雨季</u>的关系？

2. 一般来说，哪个季节比较<u>干燥</u>？干燥的季节是不是也比较<u>多风</u>？

3. 一般来说，<u>空气</u>的<u>湿度</u>在多少度人会比较舒服？

4. 你住的地区夏天比较<u>炎热</u>还是比较<u>凉快</u>？<u>湿度</u>有多高？<u>气温</u>最高多少度？

5. 你住的地区冬天比较<u>暖和</u>还是比较<u>寒冷</u>？最冷的时候气温<u>降</u>到多少度？

6. 你住的地区季节是什么样的：<u>四季分明</u>、<u>四季如春</u>，还是<u>四季如夏</u>？

U5-3.2-B　形容天气变化：忽A忽B；时A时B　[词汇 U5.7]

These two reduplicated forms are frequently used to describe fluctuating weather conditions. First read the phrases and notes below. Then complete the sentences using these expressions.

忽阴忽晴	忽高忽低	忽升忽降	忽冷忽热	时好时坏	时冷时热	时高时低
hūyīnhūqíng	hūgāohūdī	hūshēnghūjiàng	hūlěnghūrè	shíhǎoshíhuài	shílěngshírè	shígāoshídī

Note: In the above reduplicated expressions, "忽" stands for "忽然" (suddenly), and "时" for "有时候" (sometimes). The two forms "忽A忽B" and "时A时B" literally mean "suddenly A and suddenly B", or "now A, now B", suggesting fluctuating weather conditions. Both forms require antonym pairs to go with them, such as "阴—晴", "高—低", "冷—热", "好—坏", "升—降".

Listen to each sentence, then answer the question using either "**忽A忽B**" or "**时A时B**" with the *antonym* pair provided.

例：今天早上是晴天，下午变成阴天了。

　　回答问题：今天天气怎么样？（阴/晴）　　→　今天时阴时晴/今天忽阴忽晴。

1. 这个季节天气变化很大，有时好，有时坏。
   回答问题：这个季节的气候怎么样？ (好/坏)　　　　→

2. 这个星期的气温老变，昨天28度，今天就只有16度了。
   回答问题： 这个星期的气温怎么样？ (升/降)　　　→

3. 这里夏天的天气很多变，一天冷一天热的。
   回答问题： 这里夏天的天气怎么样？ (冷/热)　　　→

U5-3.2-C　形容视觉印象：成语、叠音词 ［词汇 U5.8 ］

This drill works on four-character idioms and reduplicated expressions which make your description specific and vivid.
Round 1: For each item, look at the picture and listen to the description. Then answer the question by repeating the same sentence(s).
Round 2: Read each question aloud for character recognition and answer it again with improved fluency.

例： 今天天气很好，蓝天白云，阳光灿烂。
回答问题： 今天天气怎么样？ （阴/晴）　　　　→ 今天天气很好，蓝天白云，阳光灿烂。

1. 今天天变了，阴沉沉的。
   回答问题： 今天天气怎么样？　　　　→

2. 现在外面雾蒙蒙的，开车不安全。
   回答问题： 今天你怎么不开车了？　　→

3. 一连几天都是雨绵绵的。
   回答问题：雨季的时候是什么样子？　→

4. 春暖花开的时候，这里万紫千红。
   回答问题： 这里春季有什么特点？　　→

5. 夏天很热，多半时候是夏日炎炎的。
   回答问题： 这里的夏季有什么特点？　→

6. 秋天这里很美，秋高气爽、万紫千红。
   回答问题： 这里的秋天怎么样？　　　→

7. 到处冰天雪地，白茫茫的。
   回答问题： 这里的冬天是什么样子？　→

U5-3.2-D　谈谈自己：天气与感觉 ［词汇 U5.9 ］

Round 1: Imagine you are chatting with a Chinese teacher or friend, and answer the questions by choosing appropriate expressions included in the questions.
Round 2: Read each question aloud and then answer it with improved fluency.

1. 你喜欢什么样的天气：春暖花开、烈日炎炎、秋高气爽，还是白雪茫茫、冰天雪地？
2. 什么样的天气会让你感到舒畅、精神振奋？ （蓝天白云；阴雨绵绵）
3. 什么样的天气会让你感到疲倦、郁闷、没精神：阳光灿烂、阴沉沉，还是雨绵绵的时候？

4. 你喜欢热天吗？<u>烈日炎炎</u>的时候你会有什么<u>感觉</u>？<u>精神振奋</u>还是<u>懒洋洋</u>？

5. <u>冰天雪地</u>的时候会给你什么感觉：<u>清醒</u>、<u>振奋</u>，还是<u>疲倦</u>、<u>没精神</u>？

6. 你住的地区冬天<u>气温</u>有多低？在户外会不会冷得人<u>发抖</u>、<u>手脚发僵</u>？

7. 你住的地区夏天<u>气温</u>有多高？在户外会不会热得人<u>一身是汗</u>、<u>头昏脑胀</u>？

流利强化 Fluency Enhancement

U5-3.8　语块练习：形容季节与气候特点　[词汇 U5.7-5.9]

Chunking Exercise: Listen to and repeat each phrase aloud. Then type it with 100% output accuracy. Also write all phrases by hand.

---

1. 这个季节，一年四季，这里四季分明，这里四季如春，四季如夏
2. 气候干燥，夏季闷热，雨季很潮湿，气候比较寒冷，非常温暖，特别炎热，非常凉快
3. 这几天春暖花开，蓝天白云、阳光灿烂，这几天秋高气爽，到处冰天雪地
4. 天气阴沉沉的，外面雾蒙蒙/灰蒙蒙的，这几天阴雨绵绵的，到处白茫茫的
5. 天气忽阴忽晴，气温忽高忽低，忽升忽降，天气忽冷忽热，天气时好时坏
6. 让人感到心情舒畅、精神振奋，让人感到疲倦、郁闷，没精神、懒洋洋的
7. 热得人口干舌燥、一身是汗、头昏脑胀，冷得你发抖，冷得人手脚发僵

U5-3.9　速读/巩固：《北京的四季》（5分钟）

Speed Reading/Review: Follow the steps below.

Read the text "北京的四季" in Lesson 3, focusing on meaning. Then recall as many details as possible and answer the questions.

U5-3.10　流利练习：描述气候特点和人的感觉（5分钟）

Fluency Drill: Listen to and read the following paragraph "北京的四季" sentence by sentence. Pause after each sentence for three seconds and then say the whole sentence aloud from memory. Repeat the sentence until you can say it fluently and accurately. Continue to finish the paragraph.

　　夏天大概是北京最不舒服的季节，气温有时高达<u>40多摄氏度</u>，而且比较潮湿，所以常常有一种<u>闷热</u>的感觉。天空也多半是<u>灰蒙蒙</u>的，很少能看到<u>蓝天白云</u>。有时会下一场大雨，<u>雨过天晴</u>，<u>云开日出</u>，这时天空蓝得好像是被洗干净了一样，但是气温还会很高，一出门就会<u>热得你头昏脑胀</u>、<u>一身是汗</u>。

U5-3.11　写作练习：描述气候特点（5–10分钟）

Writing Exercise: Describe the **climatic characteristics** of an area, focusing on two seasons. Provide as many details as possible using the vocabulary and expressions you have learned recently such as idioms and reduplicated adjectives. Also remember to support a general comment with specific details.

第三课·气候与感觉

第 四 课 | 灾情介绍
Lesson 4 | DISASTER REPORT

 U5-4.2 词句操练 **Aural-Oral Drills**

There are <u>three</u> drills in this lesson, which can be completed in one session (*25 min.*). You need to complete each drill twice to achieve intended results.

Important note: Before starting each drill, be sure to preview the glossary for an initial familiarization with the new words and expressions to be covered (*follow the glossary number as indicated in each drill*). For best results, also type the new words between or after the two rounds.

U5-4.2-A 表达程度 [词汇 U5.10]

This drill works on noun phrases with a modifier indicating **degree of intensity.** Listen to and read the original sentence, and then restate it adding to the <u>underlined</u> noun an adjective as hinted. In the second round, read each sentence aloud with the modifier added, with improved fluency.

(**Note:** In a formal style "的" is often omitted.)

例：这个地区发生了<u>地震</u>。　　　　(强烈)　　→　　这个地区发生了强烈<u>地震</u>。

1. 这次<u>地震</u>没有造成什么伤亡。　　(轻微)　　→
2. 去年那个地区发生了<u>旱灾</u>。　　　　(严重)　　→
3. 这个地区常常受<u>天气</u>影响。　　　　(恶劣)　　→
4. 台风给这个地区带来了<u>经济损失</u>。　(巨大)　　→
5. 这次洪水会对灾区造成<u>危害</u>。　　　(严重)　　→
6. 有关部门采取了<u>救灾措施</u>。　　　　(紧急)　　→

U5-4.2-B 词语复习：谈论灾情

This section reviews disaster-related vocabulary. Answer the following questions incorporating the provided hints. In the second round, read each sentence aloud and then answer it again with improved fluency.

1. 灾害发生以前应该做什么？　　　　　　　　　　(预防灾害发生；预防台风/暴雨袭击)
2. 灾害发生时会给灾民带来什么？　　　　　　　　(交通困难；生活上的不便)
3. 灾害发生时常常造成什么？　　　　　　　　　　(停电、停水)
4. 政府应该做什么？　　　　　　　　　　　　　　(发布警报；采取安全/预防/紧急措施；救助
   　　　　　　　　　　　　　　　　　　　　　　灾民，救援灾区)
5. 灾害发生时，灾民应该怎么办？　　　　　　　　(疏散到安全地带；离开危险地带)
6. 如果灾民不离开危险地带，会发生什么情况？　　(造成严重伤亡)
7. 灾害发生时，应该马上采取措施，先让什么恢复正常？　(交通、水电)
8. 自然灾害会使什么受到很大损失？　　　　　　　(生命财产；经济)

第
五
单
元
·
谈
论
自
然
现
象

U5-4.2-C 灾情报道：动词与常用句式 [词汇 U5.4 & 5.5; U5.10-5.12]

根据提示回答问题

This drill works on <u>ten</u> formulaic expressions and sentence patterns used in **discussing disasters** in a semi-formal or formal setting such as interviews and news reports. These expressions and structures are also applicable to other topics of cause-and-effect nature.

Round 1: Look at the formulaic sentence form or expression. Then listen to the question and answer the corresponding question(s) according to the hints provided.

Round 2: Read aloud each question for character familiarization and then answer it again with improved fluency.

例：什么时间在什么地方发生了什么
    昨晚在西南地区发生了什么? (强烈地震)　　　　→　　　昨晚在西南地区发生了强烈地震。

1. 什么时间什么灾害袭击了什么地方
   今早<u>什么</u>袭击了海南地区? (龙卷风)　　　　→

2. 什么时间什么地方(将)受到什么灾害袭击
   今明两天北方地区将<u>发生什么</u>? (受到沙尘暴袭击)　　→

3. (灾害)使_____受到严重(的)影响
   a. 洪水使<u>什么</u>受到严重的影响? (这个地区的交通)　→
   b. 这次地震使<u>什么</u>受到严重的影响? (50万居民的生活)　→

4. ……采取了_____措施
   a. 有关部门采取了<u>什么措施</u>? (紧急的救灾措施)　　→
   b. 当地政府采取了<u>什么措施</u>? (有效的防洪措施)　　→

5. 到_____为止, (灾情)已经/还没有得到控制
   a. 到今天为止，洪水的情况<u>怎么样</u>? (还没有得到控制)　→
   b. 到目前为止，山火的情况<u>还很严重</u>吗? (已经得到控制)　→

6. 据统计, 到(时间)为止……
   a. 伤亡人数有<u>多少</u>? (据统计, 到昨天为止/200多人)　→
   b. 有<u>多少人</u>无家可归? (据统计, 到目前为止/上万人)　→

7. 专家们认为, 这次灾害是(由于)_____造成的/与_____有关
   a. 这次灾害是<u>什么原因造成的</u>? (干旱和高温)　　→
   b. 这次水灾<u>与什么有关</u>? (台风和暴雨)　　→

8. 这次灾害给灾区带来/造成_____
   a. 这次台风给灾区带来<u>什么</u>? (严重的危害)　　→
   b. 这次地震给这个地区造成<u>什么</u>? (巨大的经济损失)　→

9. 据专家预测, 这次灾害 (将) 使灾区受到_____(的)损失
   a. 这次水灾使灾区受到<u>多大损失</u>? (据专家预测, ……巨大损失)　→
   b. 这次灾害使这个地区受到<u>多大的损失</u>? (……, 高达1,500万美元的经济损失) →

流利强化 Fluency Enhancement

 U5-4.7 语块练习：灾情报道 [词汇 U5.10-5.12]

Chunking Exercise: Repeat each phrase and then type it with 100% accuracy. Also select some phrases to write by hand.

1. 发生了强烈/轻微地震，　发生了严重旱灾，　受恶劣天气影响
   fāshēngle qiánglüè/qīngwēi dìzhèn　　fāshēngle yánzhònghànzāi　shòu èliètiānqì yǐngxiǎng

2. 严重/重大损失，　造成严重经济损失，　带来巨大的经济损失，　带来严重危害
   yánzhòng / zhòngdà sǔnshī　zàochéng yánzhòng jīngjìsǔnshī　dàilái jùdàde jīngjìsǔnshī　dàilái yánzhòngwēihài

3. 采取紧急措施，　采取紧急救灾/救援措施，　有关部门采取了紧急救援措施
   cǎiqǔ jǐnjícuòshī　cǎiqǔ jǐnjí jiùzāi / jiùyuán cuòshī　yǒuguānbùmén cǎiqǔle jǐnjí jiùyuáncuòshī

4. 恢复正常，　交通已经恢复正常，　得到控制，　灾情已经得到控制
   huīfùzhèngcháng　jiāotōng yǐjīng huīfùzhèngcháng　dédàokòngzhì　zāiqíng yǐjīng dédàokòngzhì

5. 交通中断，　洪水造成交通中断，　无家可归，　灾害造成上千人无家可归
   jiāotōngzhōngduàn hǒngshuǐ zàochéng jiāotōngzhōngduàn　wújiākěguī　zāihài zàochéng shàngqiānrén wújiākěguī

6. 生命财产，　生命财产受到损失，　灾害使人们的生命财产受到严重损失
   shēngmìngcáichǎn shēngmìngcáichǎn shòudàosǔnshī　zāihài shǐ rénmende shēngmìngcáichǎn shòudào yánzhòngsǔnshī

7. 与什么有关，　与暴雨有关，　这次洪水与连日暴雨有关
   yǔ shénme yǒuguān　yǔ bàoyǔ yǒuguān　zhècì hóngshuǐ yǔ liánrìbàoyǔ yǒuguān

8. 到目前为止，　伤亡人数有上千人，　到目前为止，　大部分人已经脱离危险
   dàomùqián wéizhǐ shāngwángrénshù yǒu shàngqiānrén dàomùqián wéizhǐ　dàbùfènrén yǐjīng tuōlíwēixiǎn

9. 据统计，　有10人失踪，　上万人无家可归，　据统计，　伤亡人数超过6万
   jùtǒngjì　yǒushírén shīzōng　shàngwànrén wújiākěguī　jùtǒngjì　shāngwángrénshù chāoguò liùwàn

10. 据专家预测，　据有关部门报道，　受到3亿人民币的直接经济损失
    jùzhuānjiā yùcè　jù yǒuguānbùmén bàodào　shòudào sānyì rénmínbìde zhíjiē jīngjìsǔnshī

 U5-4.8 速读/巩固：《沙尘暴的特点和危害》（3分钟）

Speed Reading/Review: Follow the steps below.
1. Read the passage within 90 seconds, focusing on meaning.
2. When you finish, recall the description details without looking at the text, and jot your notes down as quickly as possible.
3. Summarize the main points based on your notes.
4. Finally read the passage one more time to see what details you have missed.
5. Write down useful expressions for future review and practice.

沙尘暴的特点和危害

　　沙尘天气通常发生在干燥多风的春季，特点是：当有大风时，地面上的沙尘就会被风刮起，满天乱飞。自行车被刮倒，广告牌被刮掉；天的颜色变黄变暗，看不见太阳，能见度很快降低，几百米以外就会什么都看不清。所以每次起风时，路面的交通就成了很大的问题，很容易发生交通事故。风停以后，人们全身上下都是尘土，地上当然也是厚厚的一层黄土。沙尘天气期间，即使是没有大风的时候，空气中也会有细细的尘土，所以很多时候天空看上去是灰蒙蒙的。可以说，沙尘天气不但使人们的生活和工作受到很大的影响，给人们的健康带来危害，同时也给环境带来严重的问题。

U5-4.9　流利练习： 描述沙尘暴发生时的情况（5分钟）

Fluency Drill: Listen to and read "沙尘暴的特点和危害" sentence by sentence. After each sentence, pause for <u>three</u> seconds, and then say the whole sentence aloud <u>from memory</u>. Repeat a sentence until you can say it smoothly and accurately. Continue the exercise to finish the paragraph.

第 五 课
Lesson 5

比较气候、报道灾情
COMPARING CLIMATES
AND REPORTING NATURAL
DISASTERS

 U5-5.1 语段练习：介绍、比较气候特点

1. Read the text "北京的四季" in Lesson 3 closely, paying special attention to its paragraph organization and topic transitions.

2. Read the sample paragraph "昆明与北京有什么不同？" in this lesson, focusing on comparative strategies and topic transitions. **Note** also the positioning of the city name in the topic or transitional sentences.

3. Complete the exercises for introducing City A and discussing City B in comparison to Place A.

U5-5.2 词句复习：介绍气候特点

Follow the outline below for an introduction to an area's climate.

介绍气候特点	
介绍重点	简单说明四季气候特点，然后重点介绍最有特色的季节
气候特点	(很/比较/非常/特别/有点/不够……) 温和、干燥、潮湿、暖和、(炎)热、(寒)冷；多雨、多风、多雪 气温_____度；受_____影响/袭击
形容视觉 印象	蓝天白云、阳光灿烂、烈日炎炎、秋高气爽、冰天雪地、万紫千红 绿绿的、蓝蓝的、阴沉沉的、雨绵绵的、雾蒙蒙的、白雪茫茫的 蓝(绿、红、白)得像……一样
形容感觉	让人感到/觉得(很/比较/非常/特别/有点/不够)舒畅、精神振奋 疲倦、郁闷、没精神、懒洋洋的 热得人/冷得人……；头昏脑胀、口干舌燥、一身是汗；发抖、手脚发僵

单元测试与报告 Unit Assignments

For the unit review and assignments, please consult Appendices 1-3 for a guide on language use, grammar, and discourse structure.

U5-5.3 词语测试：本单元词语句式及语言结构

Vocabulary Test: Review the words and expressions in this unit and get ready for a test.

U5-5.4 课堂报告：介绍、比较两个地方的气候特点

有一个中国公司要在国外发展，你给公司介绍两个适合公司发展的地方。比较这两个地方的气候特点，并说明为什么适合公司发展。

You work for a Chinese company which is expanding its business overseas. Introduce two places in your country which might be suitable for the company's business in terms of climate. Compare the characteristics of each place to support your proposal.

U5-5.5 语段写作：报道灾害 (Choose one of the tasks)

1. 了解最近在你的国家发生过什么自然灾害，其中最严重的一次灾害是什么？按本课介绍的格式写一个简单的报道。

   Research on some recent natural disasters in your home country. Write a brief report on one of them following the format introduced in Lesson 5.

2. 根据以下示例以及灾害报道格式写一个简短的灾害报道

   Write a disaster report based on the following information, incorporating the common formulaic expressions introduced in this lesson.

时间：	2月10日		
地点：	南部地区10个省	中断	to suspend
灾害：	暴风雪	zhōngduà	
情况：	10多天低温、雨雪、冰冻	被困	be stranded
影响：	1350万人受灾；停水停电、交通中断、	běikùn	
	房屋倒塌3.5万间；80万人被困在火车站	转移	to transfer
措施：	紧急转移灾民；尽快使交通恢复正常	zhuǎnyí	
效果：	转移了175万人	气流	air current
原因：	北方冷空气和南方暖湿气流	qìliú	
后果：	死亡60人，失踪2人，经济损失60亿		

活动程序和要求 Guidelines and Instructions for the Tasks

1. 阅读讨论活动要求 Guidelines for the Reading and Discussion Activities

Your good preparation for and active participation in the class discussions are required. Follow the instructions below (unless otherwise specified by your instructor).

For reading texts: You are expected to read the text in advance as you need to answer comprehension questions and share views in class. Use a notebook or flashcards to collect useful words and expressions from the reading passages.

For your assigned task: If you have been assigned to lead a class discussion activity (by yourself or your group), you (or your group) should also prepare your activity by following these guidelines:

1) Keep your activity steps simple, clear, and efficient; do not try to accomplish too many things.
2) Limit your new vocabulary terms, if any, to five. Write the new terms on the blackboard to facilitate comprehension.
3) Have your outline, procedure, or script checked by your teacher in advance.

2. 辩论活动说明 Instructions for the Debate

辩论：应该用哪种替代能源？ Debate: Which alternative energy to use?

在太阳能、风能、水能、核能等替代能源中，应该多用哪一种，不用或少用哪一种？为什么？请具体说明理由，并提供例证。
Which alternative energy (solar, wind, water, nuclear etc.) should/should not be used? Why or why not? Present your arguments for or against a particular energy form with examples and facts.

a. 说明 Directions （选择一种辩论方式 Choose a debating format below）

方式1：专家圆桌辩论会

学生围着桌子坐（或坐成一圈），分别扮演各国／各种能源的专家，代表不同主张。老师为主持人，先简要说明各国对替代能源的需要，然后分别请各专家轮流发表看法，举例说明，并对他人看法进行反驳。（演练时须用上适当的"讨论辩论常用语"，见附录1。）

Format 1: Experts Round Table Debate
Students sit around a table (or in a circle), each playing the role of an expert from a country (or in one form of energy), representing different views. As the host, the teacher first states the need for alternative energies by various countries, and then invites each expert to take turns to express their views, give examples, and to refute the other party's views. (While role playing, use appropriate words and expressions for discussion and debate. See Appendix 1.)

方式2：分组发言

用幻灯投影报告方式。每组针对一种能源提出看法、举例说明、提供数据，并与其他能源做比较。报告的最后部分与观众（其他同学）互动，回答观众的问题。老师可请几位同学与其一起做评委，给每组报告打分并做点评。

Format 2: Group Presentation of Argument

Each group makes a slide presentation addressing a particular energy form — either in favor of or against. The presentation should include examples, facts and data as well as comparisons with other forms of energy. In the conclusion, the presenting group is expected to interact with the audience (classmates) by answering their questions. A few classmates may be invited to join the teacher to grade each presentation and give comments.

b. 辩论准备 Tips for Pre-Debate Preparations

- 每组最多3人; 可根据下面的提示先准备论点, 查阅论据和有关数据。
  Each group should include no more than three people. (*Use Worksheets at the end of the instructions.*)

- 组员分工各负责辩论/报告的一部分。
  Divide the tasks so that each member will be responsible for one part of the debate/presentation.

- 注意用本课程的词语句式，在自己中文能力范围内谈论。若翻译自己母语的演讲或作文就很可能超出了现有的中文水平。
  Remember to use appropriate vocabulary and sentence structures you have learned from this course and stay within your current proficiency level. For example, you would likely overstretch yourself if you tried to translate your speech or essay directly from your native language.

- 请注意谈论时不要深入细节, 生词请限制在8个以内（请提供生词表）。
  Also keep in mind, do NOT get into technical details in your discussion and limit the new words to eight items (provide a glossary).

- 在课堂辩论前整个小组需要先排练一下。
  Rehearse as a group before your scheduled debate/presentation. (*Use Worksheets at the end of the instructions.*)

3. 调研报告任务说明 Instructions for the Research Project

调研报告 Research Report

Work individually or in small groups on one of the following projects. Follow the guidelines below to prepare your report.

a. 介绍替代能源的开发利用

查阅你所在的国家有关使用替代能源的情况，比较目前哪一种能源利用得较多。在课上与同学交流，做简单报告，并谈自己的看法。(报告应避免太多细节和专业用语)

Reporting on the development and use of alternative energies: Do some research on the use of alternative energies in your home country. Compare the energies in terms of their current use. Then prepare a short report to present in class, and give your own comments/opinions. Avoid unnecessary details and technical terms.

b. 介绍绿色环保/节能用品

查阅办公、文具、家用、车用等环保用品，在班上做介绍。描述物品外部特征，介绍性能、用途、价格，比较其好处（与其他一般物品或节能物品相比），并谈谈自己的看法。

Introducing green/energy-saving products: Do some research to find information (with images or videos) on environmentally friendly and energy-saving products. Your presentation should include descriptions of the products' physical looks and attributes, their main features, functions, uses, and cost. Discuss their benefits compared to other regular or comparable products. Give your own opinions or comments.

c. 问卷调查报告

设计一个问卷, 并进行以下调查: 1) 同学或其他人关于全球暖化和使用替代能源的看法, 或 2) 对节能的看法、个人措施和做法。报告调查结果, 并表达自己的看法。

Survey: Design an opinion poll or survey questionnaire to find out people's opinions about the following issues: **1)** global warming and use of alternative energies, or **2)** people's views and practices with regard to green or energy-saving products. Report your survey results to the class and conclude with your own comments.

辩论准备 Debate Preparation Worksheets

1) **小组讨论/计划**

Brainstorm and Planning: List all the arguments you can think of (including those of the opposing side). Then proceed to prepare your thesis statements.

赞成开发和使用X 的理由 Arguments in Favor of X	反对开发和使用X的理由 Arguments against X
1.	1.
例子 Example:	例子 Example:
2.	2.
例子 Example:	例子 Example:
3.	3.
例子 Example:	例子 Example:
4.	4.
例子 Example:	例子 Example:
5.	5.
例子 Example:	例子 Example:

2) **组织要点**

Organize the Main Elements: Divide the tasks so that each member is responsible for one part or one point of argument (e.g., preparing supporting material). When done, integrate all materials and rehearse the debate/presentation as a group. Poster boards or graphs can be used to enhance your presentation.

引 言
Introduction
	The opening paragraph includes:
	• 例子: An opener with general information or an introduction of the main topic
	• 论点: A thesis statement. One or two sentences that includes
	  1) the main idea of the entire argument and
	  2) the main aspects to be addressed.
	
	Notes: _____
	
	_____

论 据 1 Argument 1	• 主题句: A topic sentence • 具体论据和说明: Supporting material (examples, data, etc.) Notes: _____ _____
论 据 2 Argument 2	• 主题句: A topic sentence • 具体论据和说明: Supporting material (examples, data, etc.) Notes: _____ _____
论 据 3 Argument 3	• 主题句: A topic sentence • 具体论据和说明: Supporting material (examples, data, etc.) Notes: _____ _____
结 语 Conclusion	The final part of your presentation summarizes the main points (without repeating your thesis), and may also raise new questions, make suggestions, etc. Notes: _____ _____

第六单元

UNIT **6** 谈论地理环境
TALKING ABOUT
GEOGRAPHY

第 一 课
Lesson 1

地理环境
GEOGRAPHIC
ENVIRONMENT

U6-1.2 词句操练 Aural-Oral Drills

There are **five** drills in this lesson, which can be completed in one session (*25 min.*). You need to complete each drill section twice to achieve intended results.

Important note: Before starting each drill, be sure to preview the glossary for an initial familiarization with the new words and expressions to be covered (*follow the glossary number as indicated in each drill*). For best results, also type the new words between or after the two rounds.

U6-1.2-A 谈论地理位置 [词汇 U6.0 & U6.2]

看图回答问题

This section works on the regional names and the expression "位于" for describing **geographical location**. Listen to the questions while looking at the map. Answer each question using appropriate hint provided. In the second round, repeat each question before answering it. Read the Chinese characters as well.

> 那个地方位于_____(亚洲/亚洲东部……)
> (位于wèiyú: be located, situated; lie)

1. 中国在亚洲的什么地方？ (位于亚洲的_____部)

2. 日本和韩国在中国的什么方位？ (位于中国以东、北……; 在中国的东北边……)

3. 请说出美国和加拿大的地理位置。(位于_____洲_____部)

4. 你的国家在哪个洲？ 在_____洲的哪一部分？ (位于_____洲_____部)

5. 你的国家靠近海吗？ 是哪一个海/洋？

U6-1.2-B 表达方位 [词汇 U6.2]

看图回答问题

This section works on **directional phrases** for specific locations with some areas of China. Listen to the questions while looking at the map of China, and then answer them. In the second round, repeat each question before answering it. Read the Chinese characters as well.

1. 中国在亚洲的什么地方？

2. 中国的西南部有哪几个省？

3. 西北部的哪一个省/区离北京最近？

4. 哪个地区省市比较多？ 东部还是西部？

5. 北京的位置靠近东部还是西部？

6. 上海位于中国的南部还是东部？ 靠近山还是靠近海？

7. 湖南省以南是哪两个省？ 以北呢？

8. 海南岛在广东省的南边还是北边？

9. 福建省的位置在哪两个省之间？

10. 杭州的位置靠近哪个大城市？

第
六
单
元
·
谈
论
地
理
环
境

U6-1.2-C 景物名称及量词用法 [词汇 U6.3]

看图跟读

This section works on **nouns**: monosyllabic and disyllabic (*modifier-noun compounds*). Repeat each word you hear and memorize it.

1. **单音节名词**：多用于口语；注意量词与名词的搭配

Monosyllabic Nouns are mostly used in the spoken style. **Note** the specific measure words for these nouns.

> 江　河　湖　海　山　树

Measure words:

一条江，一条河；一个湖，一个海； 一座山；一棵树

2. **复合名词**：前面的词修饰后面的名词；固定结构, 中间不能加入其他成分

Modifier-Noun Compounds: The head noun is defined by the word before it. The two parts **cannot** be separated.

> 草地　沙漠　大海　海滩　农田　雪山

Measure words:

片：一片草地、沙漠、海滩、大海、农田

座：一座雪山、高山、大山

3. **形容景物**：加形容用语使景物具体生动

Describe scenic objects vividly by adding visual impressions (*color, shape, etc.*).

一片绿绿的草地、一片黑黑的森林、一大片金色的海滩

一片绿色的农田、几座白白的雪山、一条弯弯的小河

U6-1.2-D 描述方位和景物 [词汇 U6.2-6.3]

This section works on **directional words and phrases** for **natural objects**. Follow the directions for each part.

Listen to the initial sentence carefully. Then answer the question based on the information in complete sentence.

1. 房子(的)对面是一个湖和一片农田。　　房子(的)对面是什么？　　→

2. 湖(的)周围/四周是草地和森林。　　湖(的)周围/四周是什么？　　→

3. 离村子不远的地方有一片金黄色的农田。　　离村子不远的地方有什么？　　→

Repeat the original sentence. Then construct two new sentences following the same structure and using the words provided.

4. 山和湖之间有一片黑黑的森林。

   a. 房子—树林；绿绿的草地　　→　　　房子和树林之间有一片绿绿的草地。

   b. 山—农田；金黄色的农田　　→

5. 河的两边都是树林。

   a. 湖的四周；草地　　→　　　湖的四周都是草地。

   b. 山的周围；农田　　→

6.　　那片<u>沙漠</u>(的)附近没有什么<u>村庄</u>。

　　　a. 森林；农田　　　　　　　　　→　　　　那片森林的附近没有什么农田。

　　　b. 海滩；草地　　　　　　　　　→

U6-1.2-E 问答–自述: 谈谈自己

回答完问题以后，请自己说一遍

Answer the following questions as if you were chatting with a Chinese teacher or friend. In the second round, describe the place yourself without listening to the questions.

1. 你以前住在什么城市/地区？现在呢？请说出方位：

> 在……的＿＿＿部　　　位于＿＿＿和＿＿＿之间　　　靠近＿＿＿　　　离＿＿＿不远

2. 你以前住的地方是城区还是郊区？有些什么自然景物？现在呢？

3. 你希望在你居住的地区有什么样的自然环境？(山、水、树、海滩等)

4. 你喜欢以前住的地方还是现在住的地方？为什么？

流利强化 Fluency Enhancement

U6-1.8 语块练习：方位表达 ［词汇 U6.0-6.3］

Chunking Exercise: Read each phrase aloud, and then type it out with 100% accuracy. Pinyin is not provided for this exercise.

> 1. 地理名称，地理位置，地理特征，方位，自然景物，自然资源
> 2. 位于亚洲东部，位于中国东南部，靠近太平洋，在中国以南，在欧洲和美洲地区
> 3. 靠近上海，离上海不远，在上海附近，在上海周围，在山东和山西之间
> 4. 一片黑黑的森林，一片绿绿的草地，一大片白色的海滩，一片金色的农田
> 5. 几座白白的雪山，一条弯弯的小河，几棵高大的树木
> 6. 山的对面，湖的周围，山和湖之间，离村子不远的地方，靠近海滩的地方
> 7. 山的对面是一片黑黑的森林，湖的周围是一片绿绿的草地
> 8. 沙漠附近没有草地，村庄周围有一片树林，湖的周围都是荒山，树林旁边有几个温泉

U6-1.9 速读/巩固：《中国的东西南北》　(4分钟)

Speed Reading/Review: Follow the steps below.

1. You may choose to listen to the passage once before reading, if it works for you.
2. Read the passage within <u>two</u> minutes focusing on the main ideas.
3. When you finish the first round, recall as many details as possible.
4. Read the entire passage one more time, focusing on the details.
5. Write down useful expressions for future review and practice.

U6-1.10 流利练习： 描述地理特点 (5分钟)

Fluency Drill: Listen to the following passage sentence by sentence. After each sentence, pause for <u>two</u> to <u>three</u> seconds, and then say the whole sentence aloud from memory. You should repeat each sentence until you can say the sentence smoothly and accurately with the correct tones.

　　从地图上看，中国的形状很像一只公鸡，头部是中国的东北地区，也是中国气候最冷的地方。公鸡的背部和尾部是中国北部和西部地区，这里面积广大，有雪山、草地，也有沙漠。西部也是中国海拔最高的地区，最高的地方有8848米。北部和西部面积虽然大，气候条件却不够理想，比较干燥、多风，而且由于靠近沙漠，空气受沙尘影响也比较严重。

第 二 课   **自然资源**
Lesson 2   NATURAL RESOURCES

 ## U6-2.2 词句操练 Aural-Oral Drills

There are <u>six</u> drill sections in this lesson, which can be completed in one session *(30 min.)*. You need to complete each section twice to achieve intended results.

Important note: Before starting each drill, be sure to preview the glossary for an initial familiarization with the new words and expressions to be covered (*follow the glossary number as indicated in each drill*). For best results, also type the new words between or after the two rounds.

U6-2.2-A 并列式复合名词 [词汇 U6.4]

看图跟读，回答问题

While looking at the picture(s), repeat each word you hear and try to memorize it. Then answer the questions.

注意： 下面这些词是由两个意义相近的同类名词合在一起组成的，常用于类别、整体名称，较正式；有时可拆开、扩展或缩略为单音节。

Note that two *synonymous nouns* can join together to form a *Noun-Noun Compound*, normally referring to a group, type or category of objects. They are often used in **semi-formal** or **formal** style, as well as in conversational descriptions. Sometimes these compounds can be split and expanded into a four-syllable phrase or reduced to a *monosyllabic noun*.

1. **看图跟读：** 湖泊、岛屿、海洋、江河、山岭、森林

   回答问题： 你看到了哪些景物？

2. **看图跟读：** 那里有(一些/很多/一片)森林、湖泊、岛屿

   回答问题： 那里有些什么？有没有山岭和海洋？

3. **看图跟读：** 中国有很多江河；这里有一些山岭；山上有很多花草、树木

   回答问题： 中国有很多什么？哪里有很多花草树木？

U6-2.2-B 复习自然景物名称 [词汇 U6.4-6.5]

看图跟读

While looking at the picture(s), repeat each word you hear and try to memorize it.

下面的词组是上一课学过的偏正式，每个词应该作为一个整体，不能分开。

These are *Modifier-Noun Compounds* that we covered in Lesson 1. Each word must be used as one unit (do **not** separate).

1. **看图跟读：** 沙漠、海滩、大海、高山、高原、平原、草原

   看图说出以下名词的量词： 沙漠 → 一<u>片/个</u>沙漠

   (棵)大树；(座)高山、石桥；(片/个)海滩、草地、草原

第六单元 · 谈论地理环境

U6-2.2-C 谈谈你的家乡或者你住的地区 [词汇 U6.4]

看图回答问题

Repeat each word you hear and try to memorize it. Then answer the questions.

湖泊	岛屿	海洋	江河	山岭	森林
沙漠	草原	丘陵	盆地	高原	平原

1. 你的家乡或你住的地区在哪里？

2. 那个地区有哪些地理环境和特点？

3. 那个地区**没有**哪些地理环境和特点？

4. 那个地区是在高原、平原，还是盆地？

5. 那里靠近海洋或者湖泊吗？

6. 那里靠近哪一个大洋？是在大洋的哪边？（南岸、北岸、西岸、东岸）

7. 那个地区海拔有多高？有没有3000米？

8. 那个地区多山吗？是高山还是丘陵(小山)？

9. 那个地区河流、湖泊多吗？离你们那里最近的江河、湖泊是哪一个？

10. 如果让你选择，你愿意住在靠山的地方还是靠水的地方？

U6-2.2-D 谈谈自然资源 [词汇 U6.5]

回答问题

Answer the following questions as if you were chatting with a Chinese speaker. In the second round, repeat each question before answering it. Read the Chinese characters as well.

1. 你的家乡哪方面的自然资源比较丰富？

2. 你的国家哪些地区里有矿产资源？是哪方面的矿物或产品？(煤、铜、铁，其他)

3. 你的国家出产石油和天然气吗？是哪个地区？

4. 你的国家水利资源怎么样？比如说，有没有大江大河？

5. 你的国家森林资源最丰富的地区是哪里？植物和动物资源怎么样？

6. 你的国家哪个地区的气候条件比较有利，比如说，阳光、风，等等。那里用太阳能、风能作为替代能源吗？

U6-2.2-E 数据表达 [词汇 U6.6]

The following drills work on **number expressions** and **verbs** that are commonly associated with numbers. In the second round, make sure you recognize the characters.

数字读法：跟读下面的数字

Repeat the following numbers and note the word order in the Chinese equivalents.

1. 分数：1/3 (三分之一); 2/5 (五分之二); 1/25 (二十五分之一)

2. 小数：0.2 (零点二)；20.02 (二十点零二)；2,005.28 (两千零五点二八)

3. 百分比：5% (百分之五)；25% (百分之二十五)；25.82% (百分之二十五点八二)

动词：为、占、居 (根据提示替换)

Listen to the original sentence and then substitute the **verb** with the one provided.

1. 这里的人口三分之二<u>是</u>少数民族。　　为 →　　这里的人口三分之二为少数民族。

2. 中国人口<u>有</u>世界人口的四分之一。　　占 →

3. 这里的矿产资源<u>有</u>全国的10%。　　占 →

4. 中国的人口<u>是</u>世界第一位。　　居 →

5. 那里的水利资源<u>是</u>全国第二位。　　居 →

U6-2.2-F 听读短文：《中国的地理特点》

Listen to the passage, focusing on meaning. Then answer the questions.

中国位于亚洲东部，太平洋西<u>岸</u>。中国国土面积约960万<u>平方公里</u>，约<u>占</u>亚洲<u>陆地</u>面积的<u>四分之二</u>，<u>与</u>欧洲面积<u>相似</u>，<u>居世界第三位</u>。中国地理特点是西高东低，就像三个<u>台阶</u>，从西到东，一<u>级</u>一级下降。最高的是青藏高原，<u>平均海拔</u>4000米以上，喜玛拉雅山的珠穆朗玛峰海拔8848米，是世界上最高的地方。中间的台阶海拔降到1000−2000米，<u>由</u>其他一些高原和盆地<u>组成</u>。最低的台阶海拔在500米以下，主要是平原和丘陵。由于这里的地理特点对农业有利，所以也是中国的主要<u>产粮区</u>。

回答问题

1. 中国的地理位置在哪里？
2. 面积是多少？
3. 最高的地区在哪里？有什么地理特点？
4. 最低的地区在哪里？有什么地理特点？为什么是产粮区？

岸 àn	coast, shore
面积 miànjī	area
约 yuē	approximately
平方 píngfāng	square (meter, kilometer)
公里 gōnglǐ	kilometer
占 zhàn	to take up, occupy
陆地 lùdì	dry land
四分之一 sìfēnzhīyī	one fourth
与……相似 yǔ xiāngsì	similar to...
居第三位 jū dìsānwèi	to rank third
台阶 táijiē	step
级 jí	level, step
平均 píngjūn	average
海拔 hǎibá	elevation
由……组成 yóu zǔchéng	be formed of ...
产粮区 chǎnliángqū	grain-producing area

第六单元·谈论地理环境

流利强化 Fluency Enhancement

 U6-2.8 语块练习：资源、数据表达 [词汇 U6.4-6.6]

Chunking Exercise: Read each phrase aloud, and then type it out with 100% accuracy.

1. 地理特征， 自然资源， 地形特点， 总面积， 陆地面积， 热带地区， 亚热带气候
2. 一个高原湖泊， 很多湖泊， 一条大江， 一条小河， 很多江河， 很多大江大河
3. 煤矿、金矿、铁矿， 矿泉水， 丰富的矿产资源， 丰富的水利资源， 水产品很丰富
4. 动物资源， 植物资源， 丰富的石油和天然气资源， 资源不够丰富
5. 平均海拔3000米以上， 主要是平原和丘陵， 主要是高原山区
6. 三分之一， 占总面积的三分之一， 占总人口的50%， 占全国资源的0.5%
7. 五分之二为少数民族， 四分之一为中国人， 三分之二为矿产资源
8. 居世界第一位， 居全国第三位， 在自然资源方面， 居中国第三位

U6-2.9 速读/巩固：《中国的山和水》 (5分钟)

Speed Reading/Review: Follow the steps below.

1. Read the passage "中国的山和水" in Lesson 2, focusing on meaning.
2. Without looking at the book, recall the details.
3. Read the entire passage one more time, focusing on expressions.

 U6-2.10 流利练习：描述地理特点及自然资源 (5分钟)

Fluency Drill: Listen to the entire passage once. Then listen again sentence by sentence. After each sentence, pause for <u>three</u> seconds, and then say the entire sentence aloud <u>from memory</u>. Repeat until you can say all the sentences smoothly.

> 　　中国位于亚洲东部, 太平洋西岸。中国国土面积约960万平方公里， 约占亚洲陆地面积的四分之一， 与欧洲面积相似， 居世界第三位。中国地理的特点是西高东低， 就像三个台阶， 从西到东， 一级一级下降。最低的台阶海拔在500米以下， 主要是平原和丘陵。由于这里的地理特点对农业有利， 所以也是中国的主要产粮区。

U6-2.11 写作练习：描述一个地区的地理及资源特点 (5–10分钟)

Writing Exercise: Describe an area you are familiar with or have read about. Focus on its geographic features and natural resources. Provide as many details as you can. When you are done, be sure to check your Chinese characters for accuracy.

U6-2.12 词语自测：地理环境、自然资源 (5分钟)

Vocabulary Self-Testing: Use the <u>timed memory test</u> method. Time yourself for <u>four</u> or <u>five</u> minutes to see how many words and expressions you can reproduce in the following categories. Type them out in pinyin or Chinese characters. When the time is up, also check the corresponding glossary lists to see what words you have missed.

1. Regions in the world (e.g., *continents, oceans*)
2. Directional and positional phrases (e.g., *opposite, in the vicinity of*)
3. Natural resources
4. Natural scenery (e.g., *beach, desert*)
5. Geographic features (e.g., *plateau, basin*)

第二课·自然资源

第 三 课 | **地方特色**
Lesson 3 | CHARACTERISTICS OF A PLACE

 U6-3.2 词句操练 Aural-Oral Drills

There are **nine** drills in this lesson, which can be completed in two sessions (*A-E for Session 1, 25 min., and F-I for Session 2, 20 min.*). You need to complete each drill twice to achieve intended results.

Important note: Before starting each drill, be sure to preview the glossary for an initial familiarization with the new words and expressions to be covered (*follow the glossary number as indicated in each drill*). For best results, also type the new words between or after the two rounds.

U6-3.2-A 描述印象/感觉 [词汇 U6.7]
根据提示回答问题

Read the new words aloud with comprehension. Then answer the questions using the forms and expressions in the hints provided. You are expected to recognize the Chinese characters as well.

迷人 mírén	美丽 měilì	壮观 zhuàngguān	一般 yìbān	偏僻 piānpì	边远 biānyuǎn	充足 chōngzú
贫乏 pínfá	富裕 fùyù	贫穷 pínqióng	贫困 pínkùn	发达 fādá	先进 xiānjìn	落后 luòhòu

1. 这个地方怎么样？比较富裕、先进，还是贫穷落后？ (看上去比较/有一点……)

2. 这个风景区给人什么感觉？迷人、美丽，还是很一般？ (给我的感觉是……)

3. 你怎么形容长城的景色？迷人、美丽，还是壮观？ (给人一种……的感觉)

4. 你觉得这里的风景怎么样？ (这里的风景……)

5. 你对这个地区的印象是什么？ (这个地方给我的印象是比较……)

6. 你觉得这个地方在经济上怎么样？ (看上去……)

7. 这是不是一个贫困地区？ (看上去……)

8. 这个地方的自然资源怎么样？ (给人一种……的感觉)

9. 这个地方发展太阳能怎么样？ (……给人的感觉是……很充足)

10.这个地方的交通方便吗？ (不够_____，因为比较……)

U6-3.2-B 强化表达方式：四字成语与词组 [词汇 U6.8]

根据提示改换句式

This drill works on converting **basic expressions to advanced expressions**. Repeat after the basic style, and then replace the underlined part with the phrases provided. You are expected to recognize the Chinese characters as well.

Basic Expressions	**Advanced Expressions**
	("很" is inserted for the conversational style.)
例：那个地方<u>很漂亮</u>。	风景(很)迷人 → 那个地方风景(很)迷人。
1. 那个村庄<u>在山和水的旁边</u>，<u>很美</u>。	依山傍水、风景(很)迷人 →
2. 那个地方<u>有山有水</u>，<u>很漂亮</u>。	山清水秀、风景(很)迷人 →
3. 那里是山区，<u>离城市很远</u>，<u>人很少</u>。	偏僻边远、人烟稀少 →
4. 住在这里真舒服，<u>有山有水</u>，<u>空气也很好</u>。	山清水秀、空气(很)清新 →
5. 这里只有<u>荒山荒地</u>，<u>没有花草树木</u>。	荒山野岭, 是一个不毛之地 →
6. 那里的沙漠和草原<u>非常非常大</u>。	一望无际 →
7. 秋天去看长城，山上<u>各种颜色</u>，<u>非常美</u>。	万紫千红、景色(很)壮观 →
8. 那个地方<u>离城市很远</u>，<u>也很穷</u>。	偏僻边远、贫穷落后 →
9. 这里远离城市，<u>很安静</u>，<u>风景很美</u>。	就像/是一个世外桃源 →
10. 这里<u>历史很长</u>，<u>也有很多有名的地方</u>。	……历史悠久，……名胜古迹 →

U6-3.2-C 强化表达方式：四字成语与词组 [词汇 U6.8]

跟读句子，回答问题

This section reinforces your familiarization with **four-character phrases**. For each item, listen to the initial sentence carefully and then answer the question by repeating the original sentence. Pay special attention to how four-character phrases are used in the sentences.

跟读句子	回答问题
例：那个地方的风景不错, <u>山清水秀</u>。	那个地方的风景怎么样？→那个地方的风景不错, <u>山清水秀</u>。
1. 那个地方<u>依山傍水</u>，风景很美。	那个地方有什么特点？ →
2. 这里有很多花草树木，<u>空气清新</u>。	那个地方有什么特点？ →
3. 这里秋天非常美，<u>万紫千红</u>。	秋天这里是个什么样子？ →
4. 那里<u>偏僻边远</u>，而且是一个<u>不毛之地</u>。	那个地方怎么样？ →
5. 这个地方太美了，就像一个<u>世外桃源</u>。	这个地方给你什么印象？ →
6. 那里有山有水，<u>风景非常迷人</u>。	那个地方的自然环境怎么样？ →
7. 这里从山上往下看，<u>景色非常壮观</u>。	这个地方的景色怎么样？ →
8. 那里有<u>一望无际</u>的大沙漠。	那个地方有什么特点？ →
9. 这个地方历史悠久，有很多<u>名胜古迹</u>。	这个地方给人什么印象？ →

U6-3.2-D 改换表达句式：用下面的句式替换句子

This drill works on **sentence variations** using four-character phrases. Listen to/read the original sentence. Then restate the sentence using the structure below. Recognize the Chinese characters as well.

> 那里……, 是一个＿＿＿＿＿的地方

例： 那里偏僻边远，贫穷落后。　　　　→　　　那里偏僻边远，是一个贫穷落后的地方。

1. 那里山清水秀，风景迷人。　　　　→

2. 那里依山傍水，资源丰富。　　　　→

3. 这里冬暖夏凉，四季如春。　　　　→

4. 这个地方在高原山区，阳光充足。　→

5. 这个地方贫穷落后，资源贫乏。　　→

U6-3.2-E 回答问题：谈谈自己喜欢/不喜欢的地方

Think of a place that you like/dislike and answer the questions as quickly as possible. You have only a few seconds for each question.

1. 这个地方在哪里？　　　　　　　　　(位于……, 靠近……, 离……不远)

2. 这是一个什么样的地方？　　　　　　(山清水秀、风景迷人、景色一般、空气清新、偏僻边远)

3. 这个地方有些什么自然景物？　　　　(在……有一个X)

4. 这里自然资源情况怎么样？　　　　　(丰富、贫乏、充足、稀少)

5. 这个地方是什么气候？　　　　　　　(四季分明、四季如＿＿＿＿；干燥、潮湿、多风……)

6. 为什么你喜欢/不喜欢这个地方？　　(现代、原始、贫穷落后、世外桃源、不毛之地)

U6-3.2-F 常用句型：口语转换为书面语 [词汇 U6.9]

This drill works on some expressions commonly seen in **semi-formal** and **formal** settings such as public speeches or presentations, news reporting, and expository writing.

跟读例句，并根据提示转换句式

Repeat each initial basic sentence and then the restatement using the advanced pattern/expression. Then listen to the second basic sentence and apply the advanced pattern to your restatement.

Pattern 1: ……被(人们)称为X

1) 人们**把**这个地方**叫做**"世外桃源"。　→　这个地方被称为"世外桃源"。

2) 这个地方被人们叫做"冰城"。　　　　→　这个地方被人们称为"冰城"。

Pattern 2: 由……组成

1) 这个地区是一些丘陵和盆地。 → 这个地区由一些丘陵和盆地组成。

2) 这个地方是几个小岛。 → 这个地方由几个小岛组成。

Pattern 3: 以……为主

1) 这里的自然资源主要是矿产资源。 → 这里的自然资源以矿产资源为主。

2) 这个地区主要是平原。 → 这个地区以平原为主。

Pattern 4: 以……闻名

1) 这个地方的风景很有名。 → 这个地方以风景闻名。

2) 这个地区气候寒冷是出了名的。 → 这个地区以气候冷闻名。

Pattern 5: 最……的(名词)之一

1) 这是中国一个自然资源丰富的地区。 → 这是中国自然资源最丰富的地区之一。

2) 这是中国一个特别热的地方。 → 这是中国最热的地方之一。

U6-3.2-G 表达印象常用短语 ［词汇 U6.10］

This drill works on some commonly used expressions in the conversational style. **Note:** these expressions are often used as transitional phrases, conveying a personal perspective.

听读句子，并根据提示回答问题

Listen to the original sentence focusing on the unique feature introduced. Then listen to the question and answer it in complete sentence based on the information from the initial sentence. In the second round, repeat the question before answering it.

> 在……方面很/最有特色　　最吸引人的是……　　给人印象最深的是……
>
> 美中不足的是……　　令人遗憾的是……

听读句子	回答问题	
1. 这里的山水很特别。	这里的什么很有特色？	→ 这里的山水很有特色。
2. 这里有丰富的少数民族文化。	这里什么方面最有特色？	→
3. 那里的风景很迷人。	那里最吸引人的是什么？	→
4. 这里有很多温泉。	这里最吸引人的是什么？	→
5. 这里的矿泉水特别好。	这里的什么给人印象很深？	→
6. 这个地方有很多名胜古迹。	这个地方什么给人印象最深？	→
7. 这里虽然风景很美，但比较偏僻边远。	这里令人感到遗憾的是什么？	→
8. 这里什么都好，就是交通很不方便。	这里美中不足的是什么？	→

U6-3.2-H 句型巩固

听读句子，并根据提示回答问题

This drill reinforces key **patterns/expressions** introduced earlier. Listen to the initial sentence and the question carefully. Then answer the question based on the original sentence using the pattern provided. In the second round, repeat each question before answering it.

> 以……闻名   以……为主   由……组成   占_____%   居_____位

听读句子	回答问题
1. 这个地方的<u>石油资源</u>很丰富。	这个地方的自然资源怎么样？ → (以……闻名) 这个地方以石油资源丰富闻名。
2. 在中国这里的动物资源<u>最多</u>。	这里的动物资源怎么样？ → (居全国第_____位) 这里的动物资源居全国第一位。
3. 这一带主要出产<u>水产品</u>。	这一带的经济有什么特点？ → (以……为主) 这一带的经济以水产品为主。
4. 这个地区有<u>丘陵和盆地</u>。	这个地区有什么地理特征？ → (由……组成) 这个地区由丘陵和盆地组成。
5. 这个地区有<u>一个大湖和几个小岛</u>。	这个地区有什么样的自然环境？ → (由……组成) 这个地区由一个大湖和几个小岛组成。
6. 少数民族人口有<u>地区总人口</u>的1/3。	少数民族人口是多少？ → (占) 少数民族人口占地区总人口的1/3。
7. 这里的山地有<u>地区总面积的40%</u>。	这里的山地面积是多少？ → (占) 这里的山地占地区总面积的40%。

U6-3.2-I 回答问题：谈地方特点

Answer the following questions as if you were chatting with a Chinese friend.

1. 你是哪国人？你的家乡是哪里？

2. 你的家乡的地理位置在哪里？　　　　(位于……_____部, 靠近……, 离……不远)

3. 那里有什么地理特点和自然环境？　　(高原、平原、山、江河、森林……)

4. 人口情况怎么样？　　　　　　　　　(X万, 民族以……为主, %)

5. 那个地区有多长时间的历史？　　　　(X年的历史, 很多名胜古迹)

6. 那里的气候条件怎么样？　　　　　　(一般概括+具体描述, 例子)

7. 如果我想去你们国家看看，你会推荐哪个风景区或者度假村？

8. 那个地方有什么主要特色？　　　　　(由……组成, 以……闻名, 被称为X, ……居第X位)

9. 那里还有什么其他特色，比如说食品、建筑，等等？　　(最吸引人的是……, 美中不足的是……)

10. 如果你有机会，你最想去的地方是哪里？为什么？

第六单元 · 谈论地理环境

流利强化 Fluency Enhancement

U6-3.10 语块练习

Chunking Exercise: For each item, listen to a phrase and repeat it aloud. Then type it with 100% accuracy.

U6-3.10-A 成语、常用词组 [词汇 U6.7-6.8]

1. 依山傍水的地方，山清水秀的地方，风景迷人的地方，人烟稀少的地方
2. 偏僻边远的村庄，偏僻边远的山区，一望无际的沙漠，一望无际的农田
3. 那里空气清新，那里山清水秀、风景迷人，那里的大海一望无际，景色壮观
4. 那里的秋天到处万紫千红，景色壮观，春暖花开的时候，景色非常迷人
5. 那里比较偏僻边远，比较贫穷落后，那里人烟稀少，是个不毛之地
6. 那里到处都是荒山野岭，交通不便，那里人烟稀少，空气清新，像个世外桃源
7. 这里历史悠久，有很多名胜古迹，这里气候温和，有很多风景名胜
8. 这里自然资源贫乏，比较贫穷落后，这里阳光不够充足，农业不够发达

U6-3.10-B 常用句型句式 [词汇 U6.9-6.10]

1. 把这个地方叫做"世外桃源"，把这个地方称为"世外桃源"，这个地方被称为"世外桃源"
2. 这个地区由一些丘陵和盆地组成，由一个湖和几个小岛组成，由五个少数民族组成
3. 这里的自然资源主要是矿产资源，资源以矿产资源为主，这个地区以平原为主
4. 这个地方的风景很有名，这个地方以风景闻名，这个地区以气候寒冷闻名
5. 中国自然资源最丰富的地区之一，中国最热的地方之一，最有名的风景区之一
6. 最吸引人的是这里的气候，给人印象最深的是这里的雪山风景
7. 美中不足的是这里的交通，美中不足的是气温太低，令人遗憾的是这里的食品
8. 在气候方面很有特色，在建筑方面很有特色，在饮食方面没有什么特色

U6-3.11 写作练习：描述一个景区/度假村 (10分钟)

Writing Exercise: Imagine you are writing an email to a Chinese friend. Describe a summer or winter resort you have visited. Describe your visual impressions of that place and provide as many details as possible including seasonal differences using the vocabulary and expressions you have learned in this lesson. Be sure to check your characters for accuracy.

U6-3.12 速读/巩固：《最美的地方》 (5分钟)

Speed Reading/Review: Follow the steps below.

1. Read the passage "最美的地方" in Lesson 3, focusing on meaning.
2. Without looking at the book, recall the details.
3. Read the entire passage one more time, focusing on expressions as well as sentence connection and transition.

U6-3.13 流利练习：描述自然风景 (5分钟)

Fluency Drill: Listen to the paragraph sentence by sentence. After each sentence, pause for <u>three</u> seconds, and then say the whole sentence aloud <u>from memory</u>. Repeat the sentence until you can say it smoothly and accurately. Continue the exercise to finish the paragraph. Then make a recording of the paragraph to compare with the original clip for further improvement in pronunciation and fluency.

对我来说，给我印象最深的地方是新疆，那里一望无际的大草原和有名的天山天池都很美。不过，最吸引我的是天池的景色。天池的水明净得像一面镜子，把周围雪山、树林，还有蓝天白云都映在水面上，就像一幅大自然的油画。另外，天池旁边不远的地方是大片的草地，有一个个白色的毡房，游客们可以住在那里，一面享受大自然的美景，一面还可以尝尝哈萨克人用羊奶做的奶茶、奶酒，还有奶酪。对了，他们的手抓羊肉也很有特色。美中不足的是西北的天气不够理想，那里有雪山又有沙漠，所以冬季冰天雪地，春季呢，风沙会比较大。

U6-3.14 词语自测：地区印象、地方特色 (5分钟)

Vocabulary Self-Testing: Use the <u>timed memory test</u> method. Think of two different regions or places to focus on. Then time yourself for <u>three</u> minutes to see how many adjectives and descriptive phrases (including four-character idioms and other set phrases) that you can come up with to describe each area. Type your items in pinyin or Chinese characters. When the time is up, also check your glossary lists to see what words/phrases you have missed.

Also, review the additional vocabulary terms in the three listening/reading passages in this unit. Look at the glossaries accompanying the passages and try to memorize five useful items from each passage. Then test yourself by typing them in Chinese and English with the book closed.

第 四 课 Lesson 4	**介绍地区** INTRODUCING AN AREA

U6-4.1 复习：主要句型与表达法

This review of key sentence forms, patterns and expressions serves as a quick reference guide for your writing/presentation task.

1. 主要句型与表达法 Key Sentence Patterns and Expressions

话 题 Topics	词语句式 Phrases and Sentence Forms
地理位置	位于＿＿＿＿洲＿＿＿＿部；地区；南岸
方位表达	X以东是；X 在＿＿＿＿以东；靠近Y；离Y不远；在X附近、对面、旁边
地理、环境特点	由 (几个小岛)组成；以(平原、丘陵)为主
人 口	以(汉族/少数民族)为主；X族占总人口的＿＿＿＿ %
自然资源	资源丰富/贫乏；有丰富的＿＿＿＿资源；自然资源以＿＿＿＿为主； 居全国第X位；＿＿＿＿资源占＿＿＿＿%；阳光充足；是中国最……的＿＿＿＿ 之一
风景特点	以＿＿＿＿闻名；景色迷人；山清水秀；依山傍水；景色壮观；万紫千红；像 个世外桃源；有很多风景名胜/有名的风景区；被称为……
地方特色	在＿＿＿＿方面很有特色；最吸引人的是；给人印象最深的是；美中不足的 是；令人遗憾的是；被人们称为……
出产、特产	以(农业、林业)为主；以(出产茶叶、石油)闻名；这里的出产主要包括X、Y和 Z，其中Y……

2. 关联词与连接性词语 Sentence Connectors and Transitional Phrases

从……上看	在……方面
因为……所以	虽然……但(是)
另外, 这里的＿＿＿＿也……不一样	
除了X以外, Y也很有特色	

单元测试与报告 Unit Assignments

For the unit review and assignments, please consult Appendices 1-3 for a guide on language use, grammar, and discourse structure.

U6-4.4 词语测试：本单元词语句式及语言结构

Vocabulary Test : Review the words and expressions in this unit and complete the online or written test assigned by your teacher.

U6-4.5 报告：介绍中国西部一个地区

(个人或小组)查阅资料，了解一个中国西部省区的情况，如一个西南、西北的省或少数民族自治区。准备一个简单报告，包括下面表格中所列出的各项。在准备报告前请复习第四课语段组织要点。

Work individually or in small groups. Research on a province or region in western China, e.g., a southwestern or southeastern province or a minority autonomous area. Prepare a short report presenting the information as listed in the following data worksheet. Review the tips for **paragraph organization** in Lesson 4 thoroughly to prepare your report.

	例子 Example	资料 Data/Notes
名 称	云南省	
位 置	西南部 北：四川 西北：西藏 东：贵州、广西	
地 理 特 点	高原、盆地、高山、河流、湖泊、森林	
气 候	温和、潮湿；夏季平均气温18-20度；冬季……	
资 源	矿产(有色金属)、森林、动物、植物、水利、风景区等	
人 口	(2002年)4288万；少数民族约1360万(全国第二位)	
出 产/特 产	茶叶、烟、大理石、木材、药材等	
其 他		

活动程序和要求 Guidelines and Instructions for the Tasks

1. 阅读讨论活动要求 Guidelines for the Reading and Discussion Activities

Your good preparation for and active participation in the class discussions are required. Follow the instructions below (unless otherwise specified by your instructor).

For reading texts: You are expected to read the text in advance as you need to answer comprehension questions and share views in class. You can use a notebook or flashcards to collect useful words and expressions from the reading passages.

For your assigned task: If you have been assigned to lead a class discussion activity (by yourself or your group), you (or your group) should also prepare your activity by following these guidelines:

1) Keep your activity steps simple, clear, and efficient; do not try to accomplish too many things.
2) Limit your new vocabulary terms, if any, to <u>eight</u>. Write the new terms on the blackboard to facilitate comprehension.
3) Have your outline, procedure, or script checked by your teacher in advance.

2. 情景模拟任务准备 Preparing for the Simulation Tasks

The following simulation tasks focus on presentation of an area's profile, geographic information, and natural sceneries. You are also expected to demonstrate your communicational skills through your interactions with the audience. Be sure to review four-character idioms and other common phrases, key sentence patterns and expressions, and paragraph organization tips in preparing these tasks. A preparation worksheet is provided below for your use.

选一个模拟情景 (Choose one of the scenarios)

任务1：介绍风景名胜/旅游景点 Introducing Famous Scenic Resorts/Tourist Spots

角 色 Roles	外国旅游公司代表（2–3人），观众（其他同学） Travel agents (2-3), audience (played by other classmates)
情景/任务 Scenario/Task	你们代表你们国家的一个旅游公司，想让中国人到你们国家去旅游。在一个产品展销会上你们向大家介绍你们国家的风景区，并回答大家的问题。 You are representatives of a major travel agency in your home country and are promoting your tourist business in the Chinese market. At an international trade fair you present some famous resorts and tourist spots and interact with the audience (played by your classmates) by showing brochures and pictures as well as answering their questions.
要 求 Requirements	时间长度: 8–10分钟。模拟表演分为2段，先做介绍，然后与观众互动。可用幻灯投影、图片板、地图、说明书等，但不能用稿子或提示卡。多用学过的词语句式；生词应限制在5个以内。准备时请先复习成语及常用词组、句型句式，以及段落要点。 Time limit: 8-10 minutes for the simulation. The simulation consists of two parts: a presentation session and a Q&A session to interact with the audience. You can use slides, poster boards, maps, or brochures to enhance your presentation. However, you are not allowed to read from your script or an index card. Use vocabulary and structures recently covered and limit your new words to five items. Before your presentation, review four-character idioms, common set phrases, sentence structures, and paragraph organization tips.

评 估 Presentation	老师可邀请同学做评委一起给每个表演的小组打分, 选出最佳表演。 Your teacher may ask some of you to grade each group's performance and vote for the best presentation.

任务2: 吸引投资人　Attracting Investors

角 色 Roles	大学毕业生（2–3人）, 投资商（其他同学扮演） College graduates studying in China (2-3), potential investors (played by other classmates)
情景/任务 Scenario/Task	在中国期间, 你们旅游了很多地方, 发现有一个地方的风景非常好, 可以发展旅游业。你们想在这里建一个度假村, 但需要资金。有几个投资商有兴趣。你们向投资商介绍这个地区的情况、想像的度假村是什么样子、会给地区和投资商带来什么好处等; 也要回答投资商的问题。 During your stay in China you have traveled to many places. One place has impressed you the most by its beautiful scenery, which is perfect for tourism. You plan to build a vacation resort there, but need funding. Some potential investors would like to hear your proposal. Your task is to sell your ideas: present this area's profile, its geographic advantages and natural resources; describe the proposed resort, and explain the potential benefits to the area as well as to the investors. Also answer the investors' queries.
要 求 Requirements	时间长度: 8–10分钟。模拟表演分为2段, 先做介绍, 然后与投资人互动。可用幻灯投影、草图、图片板、地图等, 但不能用稿子或提示卡。多用学过的词语句式; 生词应限制在5个以内。准备时请先复习成语及常用词组、句型句式, 以及段落要点。 Time limit: 8-10 minutes. The simulation consists of two parts: a presentation session and a Q&A session to interact with the investors. You can use slides, sketches, poster boards, or maps to enhance your presentation. However, you are not allowed to read from your script or from an index card. Use vocabulary and structures recently covered and limit your new words to five items. Before your presentation, review four-character idioms, common set phrases, sentence structures, and paragraph organization tips.
评 估 Presentation	老师可邀请同学做评委一起给每个表演的小组打分, 选出最佳表演。 Your teacher may ask some of you to grade each group's performance and vote for the best presentation.

介绍地区特点 Preparation Worksheet

Use this worksheet as a rough guide for the coverage of information.

地区名称	
地理位置	
地理特点	
气候特点	
自然环境	
风景/资源等特色	
其他特点	

3. 定时写作任务说明 Instructions on the Timed Composition

Complete this writing task within **20 minutes**. Your composition should be at least two paragraphs, with general statements and supporting details and examples. Include the following information as you see fit to make your descriptions substantial.

你的两个中国朋友想到你们国家来旅游，问你去哪里比较好。你给他们介绍两个有名的风景区或度假村。你的介绍应该具体详细，包括地区名称、地理位置、地理特点、气候情况、自然环境、自然资源和风景等情况。

Two Chinese friends want to visit your home country, and ask for your recommendations. You introduce two famous places (national parks or vacation resorts). Your introduction should be specific and detailed, including the name of the area, its geographic location and characteristics, weather, natural environment, natural resources, sceneries, and other related information.

第七单元	谈论城市	第 一 课	城市设施
U N I T 7	TALKING ABOUT CITIES	Lesson 1	IN THE CITY

 U7-1.2 词句操练 Aural-Oral Drills

There are <u>four</u> drills in this lesson, which can be completed in one session (*25 min.*). You need to complete each drill section twice to achieve intended results.

Important note: Before starting each drill, be sure to preview the glossary for an initial familiarization with the new words and expressions to be covered (*follow the glossary number as indicated in each drill*). For best results, also type the new words between or after the two rounds.

U7-1.2-A 城市设施 [词汇 U7.2]

看图跟读并回答问题

While looking at the picture(s), repeat each word you hear and try to memorize it. Then answer the questions.

跟读：这里有一个/家(银行) 。   回答问题：这里有什么？

U7-1.2-B 方位表达 [词汇 U7.1-7.2]

根据所给的句式和提示回答问题

This section works on common terms for **urban facilities** while drilling the usage of "**就有**" and "**就是**". Please see the notes and examples under "**Forms and Structures**" in the Textbook for details.

Answer each question using the "就有" or "就是" form. In the second round, repeat the question aloud before answering it. You are expected to recognize the Chinese characters as well.

> (方位/地点) 就有/就是一个 (餐馆)
>
> There is (a restaurant) right there at (location).

例: 请问<u>这附近</u>有没有西餐馆？	(街对面)	→	<u>街对面就有</u>一个西餐馆。
1. 您知道<u>附近</u>哪里有一个购物中心？	(电影院那里)	→	电影院那里<u>就有</u>一个……
2. 请问<u>这附近</u>有邮局吗？	(购物中心对面)	→	购物中心对面<u>就是</u>一个……
3. 麻烦您，<u>哪里</u>有一个外文书店？	(天桥下面)	→	天桥下面<u>就有</u>一个……

> (你要找的地方) 就在 (方位/地点)
>
> (The place you are looking for) is right at (location).

例: 请问<u>中国银行</u>在哪儿？	(大华超市旁边)	→	(中国银行)<u>就在</u>大华超市旁边。
1. 请问<u>历史博物馆</u>是在附近吧？	(那栋楼对面)	→	历史博物馆就在……
2. 麻烦您，"<u>天天来小吃店</u>"在哪儿？	(立交桥旁边)	→	"天天来小吃店" 就在……
3. 请问，<u>停车场</u>在哪里？	(那个报摊前面)	→	停车场就在……

U7-1.2-C 扩展词语：方位表达为修饰语
根据所给的句式和提示回答问题

This drill works on **locative phrases** used as a modifier. Answer each question following the hint provided. In the second round, repeat the question aloud before answering it. You are expected to recognize the Chinese characters as well.

> 就是(方位/地点)的那个……

Note: Here "就是" is used for clarification, meaning "(It's) the one that..."

例: 你去的是哪个中国银行？　　(大华超市旁边)　　→　　就是大华超市旁边的那个(中国银行)。

1. 你说的是哪个停车场？　　　(购物中心旁边)　　→

2. 你想去哪个西餐馆？　　　　(中国银行对面)　　→

3. 你上次住的是哪个酒店？　　(星巴克后面)　　→

U7-1.2-D 回答–自述 [词汇 U7.0-7.3]
先回答问题, 然后练习自述; 准备在课上和同学交流

Answer the following questions as if you were chatting with a Chinese teacher or friend. In the second round, repeat each question before answering it. You are expected to read the characters as well.

1. 在你住过的城市里，你最喜欢的是哪一个？

2. 请说出这个城市的地理位置。(位于_____国_____部, 靠近……, 在……附近/在X与Y之间)

3. 这个城市有些什么设施？(医院、宾馆、机场……)

4. 那里的商业区在哪里？(位于……, 靠近……/在……附近)

5. 你常去哪些地方？

6. 如果你的朋友来了，你会带他/她去哪些地方？(一个___餐馆, 在……)

7. 为什么你选择那几个地方？

流利强化 Fluency Enhancement

U7-1.9 语块练习：城区景物方位表达 [词汇 U7.0-7.3]

Chunking Exercise: Listen to and repeat the phrases aloud. Then type them with 100% accuracy.

1. 住在城区，　住在郊区，　现代化的社区，　热闹的商务区，　安静的住宅区
   zhùzài chéngqū　zhùzàijiāoqū　xiàndàihuàde shèqū　rènaode shāngwùqū　ānjìngde zhùzháiqū

2. 公共设施，　餐饮娱乐，　公交系统，　高速公路，　很窄的街道
   gōnggòngshèshī　cānyǐnyúlè　gōngjiāoxìtǒng　gāosùgōnglù　hěnzhǎide jiēdào

3. 大型超市，　大型商场，　中小型机场，　大型购物中心
   dàxíngchāoshì　dàxíngshāngchǎng　zhōngxiǎoxíng jīchǎng　dàxíng gòuwùzhōngxīn

4. 对面就有一个停车场，　附近就有一个麦当劳，　车站旁边就有几个快餐店
　　duìmiàn jiùyǒu yígè tíngchēchǎng　　fùjìn jiùyǒu yígè màidāngláo　　chēzhàn pángbiān jiùyǒu jǐgè kuàicāndiàn

5. 西餐厅就在宾馆附近，　肯德基就在那家电影院对面，　网吧就在歌舞厅下面
　　xīcāntīng jiùzài bīnguǎn fùjìn　　kěndéjī jiùzài nàjiā diànyǐngyuàn duìmiàn　　wǎngbā jiùzài gēwǔtīng xiàmiàn

6. 一家不错的小吃店，　很有特色的风味餐厅，　普通的咖啡馆，　便宜的快餐店
　　yìjiā búcuòde xiǎochīdiàn　　hěnyǒu tèsède fēngwèicāntīng　　pǔtōngde kāfēiguǎn　　piányide kuàicāndiàn

7. 邮局附近的那个商店，　机场附近的那个体育场，　博物馆斜对面的那个健身房
　　yóujú fùjìnde nàgè shāngdiàn　　jīchǎng fùjìnde nàgè tǐyùchǎng　　bówùguǎn xiéduìmiànde nàgè jiànshēnfáng

8. 在广场附近的那个饭店住，　在地铁站旁边的那个餐馆吃饭，
　　zài guǎngchǎngfùjìnde nàgèfàndiàn zhù　　zài dìtiězhàn pángbiānde nàgè cānguǎn chīfàn

　　在星巴克对面的那个酒楼请客
　　zài xīngbākè duìmiànde nàgè jiǔlóu qǐngkè

U7-1.10 速读/巩固：《中国的城市发展与变化》（4分钟）

Speed Reading/Review: Follow the steps below.

1. Read the passages about "中国的城市发展变化" in Lesson 1, focusing on words and expressions.
2. Without looking at the book, recall the details in Chinese.
3. Read the passage again. Learn the new words and useful expressions.

U7-1.11 流利练习：描述城市变化（5分钟)

Fluency Drill: Listen to the following lines from the reading passage. After each sentence, pause for two to three seconds, and then repeat the whole sentence aloud from memory. You should repeat each sentence until you can say the sentence smoothly and accurately with the correct tones.

　　自从80年代中国改革开放以来，中国的城市发生了巨大的变化。从外观上看，以前低矮的老式建筑都不见了，商业区和住宅区里到处都是现代的高楼大厦。商店也有很大的变化。以前商店都是国有企业，最大的商店称为"百货商店"。一般来说，一个城市里只有两三家百货商店，小城市里往往就只有一家。那时商品的品种款式都很少，很多时候购物还得排队，甚至得凭票证购买棉布、自行车、电视机等物品。90年代以后，私营的大型商场和购物中心越来越多，包括外国的沃尔玛、家乐福这样的大型超市。另外，餐饮业的变化也很大。从前城市里的餐馆以当地的食物为主，而现在每个城市里不但有中国各地的风味餐厅，而且也有外国的快餐店、咖啡馆，如麦当劳、星　巴克等。可以说，现在的中国城市越来越国际化了。

第 二 课 | 城区特点
Lesson 2 | URBAN CHARACTERISTICS

 U7-2.2　词句操练 Aural-Oral Drills

There are **four** drill sections in this lesson, which can be completed in one session (*20 min.*) You need to complete each section twice to achieve intended results.

Important note: Before starting each drill, be sure to preview the glossary for an initial familiarization with the new words and expressions to be covered (*follow the glossary number as indicated in each drill*). For best results, also type the new words between or after the two rounds.

U7-2.2-A 数字表达：多位数怎么读和写 [词汇 U7.4]

This drill works on reading and writing of **big numbers** (see notes and examples under "**Forms and Structures**" in Lesson 2 in the Textbook).

先跟读，然后回答问题

For each item, repeat the original expression. Then answer the question based on this initial information.

1. Basic measure words

个 (1)　　　十 (10)　　　百 (100)　　　千 (1,000)　　　万 (10,000)　　　亿 (100,000,000)

2. The "万-Group" (starting from the fifth digit through the eighth digit)

万　　　十万 (10万)　　　百万 (100万)　　　千万 (1000万)

	Example	Read as...	Written as...
1 0,000　(1万)	2 0,500	两万零五百	20500 或 2.05万
10 0,000 (10万)	20 5,000	二十万零五千	20.5万
1,00 0,000 (100万)	2,20 5,000	二百二十万零五千	220.5万
10,00 0,000 (1000万)	22,05 0,000	二千二百零五万	2205万

3. The "亿-Group" (starting from the ninth digit through the twelfth digit)

亿　　　十亿 (10亿)　　　百亿 (100亿)　　　千亿 (1000亿)

	Example	Read as...	Written as...
1 00,000 0,000 (1亿)	2 20,000 0,000	两亿二千万	2.2亿
1,0 00,000 0,000 (10亿)	2,2 00,000 0,000	二十二亿	22亿
10,0 00,000 0,000 (100亿)	22,0 00,000 0,000	二百二十亿	220亿
100,0 00,000 0,000 (1000亿)	220,0 00, 00 0,000	二千二百亿	2,200亿

U7-2.2-B 谈城市印象 ［词汇 U7.5-7.6］

谈城市印象

Answer the questions based on the pictures. In the second round, repeat each question before answering it.

1. 这是什么区？住宅区还是商业区？

2. 这里的建筑有什么特色？是现代建筑还是传统建筑？

3. 这个城市的市容怎么样？干净整洁还是比较脏乱？

4. 这个城市的交通状况怎么样？街道上拥挤吗？

5. 造成拥挤的主要原因是什么？车辆还是行人？

6. 你觉得这里的治安情况怎么样？

7. 你觉得这里的生活节奏怎么样？比较快还是比较慢？

8. 你觉得这里比较安静还是比较吵？为什么？

9. 这个地方比较吸引人的是哪些方面？为什么？(用名词和形容词)

10. 你对这个城市的印象是什么？用哪些形容词描述比较合适？

U7-2.2-C 做比较：相似还是不同

回答问题

Compare the cities you have just viewed. Listen to each question followed by the choices, and then repeat the most suitable answer.

> A和B很相似/很不同　　A不如B(好)　　A比B更……　　A和B一样

1. 你所在的城市和这个中国城市很相似还是很不同？

2. 两个城市相比，在市容方面……(哪一句合适？)

   1) 这个城市不如我所在的城市干净整洁。　2) 这个城市和我所在的城市一样干净整洁。

   3) 这个城市比我所在的城市更脏乱。　　　4) 这两个城市都不够干净整洁。

3. 两个城市相比，在城市建筑方面……(哪一句合适？)

   1) 这个城市的高楼大厦不如我所在的城市的漂亮。

   2) 这个城市的高楼大厦比我所在的城市的更漂亮。

   3) 这个城市的高楼大厦和我所在的城市的很相似。

   4) 这两个城市都不够漂亮。

4. 你所在的城市和这个中国城市比起来怎么样？

   1) 哪个城市比较拥挤？　　　　　　　2) 哪个城市的车辆行人多？

   3) 哪个城市比较先进发达？　　　　　4) 哪个城市看上去比较现代？

   5) 哪个城市的发展看上去比较迅速？

U7-2.2-D 谈谈你对城市生活的看法

回答下面的问题，并准备好在课上做调查

Answer the following **survey questions** by choosing appropriate answers from the list provided. In the second round, repeat each question before answering it. (Be prepared to interview your classmates in class.)

1. 你希望住在什么样的城市？　　　　　　　　　(热闹、快节奏的大城市,节奏慢一点的中小城市)

2. 你认为住在城市里的最大好处是什么？　　　　(购物方便,生活丰富,热闹,餐馆多,交通方便)

3. 周末你比较想去什么地方？　　　　　　　　　(娱乐场所,餐馆,健身中心,购物中心,博物馆)

4. 什么会给城市带来最不好的影响？　　　　　　(无业游民,游客,垃圾,噪音,污染,车辆)

5. 如果你是一个城市居民，什么对你最重要？　　(街道整洁,商业发达,交通方便,治安良好)

6. 如果城区公共交通方便，你会用什么方式上班？(自己开车,用公交车或地铁,骑自行车)

7. 哪一个情况会让你最受不了？　　　　　　　　(街道脏乱,交通不便,购物不便,健身不便,噪音大)

8. 选择一个城市居住，哪些原因最重要？　　　　(家人/婚恋,气候,工作机会,历史文化,生活条件)

9. 选择一个城市居住，哪一个原因最<u>不</u>重要？　 (家人/婚恋,气候,工作机会,历史文化,生活条件)

10. 你对你所在的城市哪方面不够满意？　　　　　(市容,交通,娱乐,治安,旅游,其他)

U7-2.2-E 动词：增长、增加、上升

根据提示回答问题

Answer the question based on the data/information provided, note the verbs used for the particular nouns. In the second round, repeat each question aloud before answering it, and recognize the Chinese characters as well.

> **Note** the difference in meaning and usage:
> 1. "增长" (to grow, increase): It is associated with growth in general terms and is normally represented by rates, fractions or large numbers. It typically refers to "growth" at a certain rate (e.g., economic, population). The opposite is "负增长" (负 fù / negative).
> 2. "增加" (to add, increase): It is usually related to quantity and concrete numbers. The opposite is "减少"(jiǎnshǎo).
> 3. "上升" (to rise, ascend): It also uses percentage rates to indicate degrees of increase. The subject or topic of "上升" normally refers to a number or rate that is expected to fluctuate (e.g., enrollment, index, price or value). The opposite is "下降", and both words are often abbreviated as "升/降".

例: 这10年里, 这里的人口增长了多少？　　　(2%)　　　→　　　人口增长了2%。

1. 和去年相比，今年的经济增长了多少？　　(8%)　　　→　　　今年的经济增长了8%。

2. 这个城市的人口增长速度怎么样？　　　　(很迅速)　→　　　人口增长得很迅速。

3. 今年这个大学的新生人数增加了吗？　　　(+150)　　→　　　增加了150名。

4. 去年高校毕业生人数上升了多少？　　　　(+20%)　　→　　　去年人数上升了20%。

5. 毕业人数增加了，就业机会也增加了吗？　(-)　　　　→　　　没有，就业机会减少了。

6. 今年房子价格比去年上升了还是下降了？　(- 2%)　　→　　　今年房价下降了2%。

流利强化 Fluency Enhancement

U7-2.9 语块练习：形容城区状况 ［词汇 U7.4-7.6］

Chunking Exercise: Listen to and repeat the phrases aloud. Then type them with 100% accuracy.

1. 2万辆车， 20万游客， 200万流动人口， 2000万居民， 2亿人口
   liǎngwànliàngchē èrshíwàn yóukè liǎngbǎiwàn liúdòng rénkǒu liǎngqiānwàn jūmín liǎngyì rénkǒu

2. 流动人口太多， 无业游民不少， 街上行人很多， 人口密度很大
   liúdòng rénkǒu tàiduō wúyè yóumín bùshǎo jiēshang xíngrén hěnduō rénkǒu mìdù hěndà

3. 看上去比较先进发达， 看上去不够现代， 看上去比较落后
   kànshàngqu bǐjiào xiānjìnfādá kànshàngqu búgòuxiàndài kànshàngqu bǐjiàoluòhòu

4. 商店里有点冷清， 娱乐场所非常热闹， 房子比较破旧， 街道有点脏乱
   shāngdiànli yǒudiǎn lěngqīng yúlèchǎngsuǒ fēichángrènao fángzi bǐjiào pòjiù jiēdào yǒudiǎn zāngluàn

5. 发展迅速， 发展缓慢， 生活节奏比较慢， 车辆很多， 交通非常拥挤
   fāzhǎnxùnsù fāzhǎnhuǎnmàn shēnghuójiézòu bǐjiàomàn chēliànghěnduō jiāotōng fēicháng yōngjǐ

6. 繁华热闹的城市， 繁华热闹的商业区， 到处是高楼大厦， 很多现代建筑
   fánhuárènaode chéngshì fánhuárènaode shāngyèqū dàochù shì gāolóudàshà hěnduō xiàndàijiànzhù

7. 市容不够干净整洁， 治安不够好， 街道上比较拥挤， 噪音很大， 空气污染严重
   shìróng búgòu gānjìngzhěngjié zhì'ān búgòuhǎo jiēdàoshang bǐjiào yōngjǐ zàoyīn hěndà kōngqìwūrǎn yánzhòng

8. 社区整整洁洁， 街道上干干净净， 车站里热热闹闹， 这个商店里冷冷清清
   shèqū zhěngzhěngjiéjié jiēdàoshang gāngānjìngjìng chēzhànli rèrènaonao zhège shāngdiànli lěnglěngqīngqīng

U7-2.10 速读/巩固：《中国的城市人口》(3分钟)

Speed Reading/Review: Follow the steps below.

1. Read the passage "中国的城市人口" in Lesson 2, focusing on words and expressions.
2. Without looking at the book, recall the details in Chinese.
3. Read the passages again and learn the new words and useful expressions.

U7-2.11 写作练习：描述城区印象

Writing Exercise: Imagine you are writing an email to a friend about your visit to a city for the first time. Describe the city and tell your friend why you like or dislike it. Provide as many details as you can using the vocabulary and sentence forms recently covered. When done, be sure to check your Chinese characters for accuracy.

U7-2.12 词语自测：城市设施、城区特点 (5分钟)

Vocabulary Self-Testing: Use the timed memory test method. Time yourself for three minutes to see how many words and expressions you can reproduce in the following categories. Type them out in pinyin or Chinese characters. When the time is up, also check the glossary lists to see what you have missed.

1. Facilities and objects in the city (e.g., *bank, mall, overpass*...)
2. Nouns associated with urban life (e.g., *garbage, noise, residential area*...)
3. Adjectives for urban characteristics (e.g., *advanced, modern, noisy*...)

第 三 课 | **城市发展与变化**
Lesson 3 | CHANGES AND DEVELOPMENT OF A CITY

 U7-3.2 词句操练 Aural-Oral Drills

There are <u>eight</u> drills in this lesson, which can be completed in two sessions *(A-D, and E-H; 25 min. each)*. You need to complete each drill twice to achieve intended results.

Important note: Before starting each drill, be sure to preview the glossary for an initial familiarization with the new words and expressions to be covered *(follow the glossary number as indicated in each drill)*. For best results, also type the new words between or after the two rounds.

U7-3.2-A 成语及常用词组 [词汇 U7.7]
跟读并回答问题

Repeat the initial sentence. Then answer the question based on the information.

高楼大厦	四通八达	五光十色	灯火辉煌	繁华热闹	应有尽有	名胜古迹
gāolóudàshà	sìtōngbādá	wǔguāngshísè	dēnghuǒhuīhuáng	fánhuárènao	yīngyǒujìnyǒu	míngshènggǔjì

看图跟读	回答问题
1. 这个城市看上去很现代，到处都是<u>高楼大厦</u>。	这个城市是什么样子？
2. 这个城市新建的高速公路<u>四通八达</u>。	这个城市新建的高速公路怎么样？
3. 这条街<u>繁华热闹</u>，各种商店<u>应有尽有</u>。	这条街有什么特点？
4. 这个城市<u>先进发达</u>，给人的感觉是一个现代化城市。	这个城市怎么样？
5. 过年过节时这里非常漂亮，<u>五光十色</u>，<u>灯火辉煌</u>。	过年过节时这里是什么样子？
6. 这里是<u>历史名城</u>，有很多<u>名胜古迹</u>，所以游客很多。	这里为什么游客很多？

交通堵塞	人来人往	冷冷清清	垃圾成堆	民族特色	文化气息	历史悠久
jiāotōngdǔsè	rénláirénwǎng	lěnglěngqīngqīng	lājīchéngduī	mínzútèsè	wénhuàqìxī	lìshǐyōujiǔ

看图跟读	回答问题
1. 上下班的时间路上车辆很拥挤，常常造成<u>交通堵塞</u>。	车辆拥挤时会造成什么？
2. 这条街很热闹，<u>人来人往</u>，而旁边那条街却<u>冷冷清清</u>。	这两条街有什么不同？
3. 这个城市的市容不好，又脏又乱，<u>垃圾成堆</u>。	为什么说这里市容不好？
4. 这里少数民族比较多，餐馆里的食品很<u>有民族特色</u>。	这里的食品有什么特点？
5. 这一带是大学区，附近也有音乐厅和博物馆，<u>很有文化气息</u>。	这里有什么特点？
6. 这个城市<u>历史悠久</u>，所以<u>文化气息</u>非常浓厚。	这是一个什么样的城市？

U7-3.2-B 描述印象/感觉：四字成语与词组 ［词汇 U7.7］
根据提示回答问题，并用上所给的句式

This drill works on descriptions of one's dominant **impressions of a city**. Answer the questions using an appropriate sentence form listed in the box and the hinted phrases following each question. In the second round, repeat the question aloud before answering it. You are expected to recognize the Chinese characters as well.

> 看上去……， 给人的印象/感觉是……， 给人一种……的感觉

1. 这个城市给你什么印象？ （高楼大厦； 先进发达）
   → 这里到处都是<u>高楼大厦</u>，<u>看上去</u>比较<u>先进发达</u>。

2. 这个商店给你什么感觉？ （人来人往；商业发达） →

3. 你觉得这个市场怎么样？ （物品很多；应有尽有） →

4. 这个商店怎么样？ （服装、饰品，花花绿绿；民族特色） →

5. 这条街给你什么感觉？ （书店、博物馆；文化气息） →

U7-3.2-C 形容用语 ［词汇 U7.7］
改换说法：一般表达转换为成语和常用词组

There are some basic and advanced expressions. Listen to or read the original sentence, and then restate it with the four character idioms and phrases provided as shown in the examples. In the second round, say both basic and advanced sentences aloud, and recognize the Chinese characters as well.

Basic Expressions		Advanced Expressions
		("很" is inserted for the conversational style.)
例： 这个城市的交通很方便。	(四通……) →	这个城市的交通<u>四通八达</u>。
1. 这个车站车很多，<u>哪里都可以去</u>。	(四通……) →	这个车站四通八达。
2. 过年的时候商店里<u>装饰得非常漂亮</u>。	(五光……) →	过年的时候商店里五光十色。
3. 广场周围都是<u>很高的楼</u>。	(高楼……) →	广场周围都是高楼大厦。
4. 这是一个亚洲有名的<u>最高的楼</u>。	(摩天……) →	这是一个亚洲有名的摩天大楼。
5. 北京有很多<u>历史和文化上有名的地方</u>。	(名胜……) →	北京有很多名胜古迹。
6. 这条街很热闹，总是<u>有很多人</u>。	(人来……) →	这条街很热闹，总是人来人往。
7. 过年过节的时候，这里的<u>灯很亮</u>，<u>很漂亮</u>。	(灯火……) →	过年过节的时候，这里灯火辉煌。
8. 这里经济发展很好，<u>商店多</u>，<u>购物的人也多</u>。	(繁华……) →	这里经济发展很好，繁华热闹。
9. 这个城市<u>有很长的历史</u>。	(……悠久) →	这个城市历史悠久。

第七单元 · 谈论城市

U7-3.2-D 回答问题：谈谈自己熟悉的城市

About a Familiar City: Let's chat about an urban area you are familiar with. Answer the questions as if you were sharing cultural information with a group of people with diverse cultural background.

1. 你认为世界上最繁华热闹的城市是哪几个？(请说三个)

2. 在你的国家，最先进发达的城市是哪几个？(请说两个)

3. 你认为中国城市里，商业最发达的是哪几个？

4. 你知道除了北京以外，哪几个中国城市的名胜古迹比较多？

5. 在你的国家，哪几个城市是历史名城：历史最悠久，名胜古迹比较多？

6. 在你的国家，城市交通怎么样？是不是经常有交通堵塞的情况？

7. 在你的国家，城市多半比较干净整洁还是比较脏乱？有没有垃圾成堆的情况？

8. 哪个城市最有文化气息？(比如说，有书店、学校、博物馆、艺术品等)

Please be prepared to share information in a class activity.

9. 如果请你介绍一个你最喜欢的城市，你会怎么介绍这个城市的主要特色？有什么具体的例子？

10.除了主要特色以外，你能不能告诉我们这个城市的其他情况：气候、旅游景点、宾馆价格、餐馆价格、买什么礼物？

U7-3.2-E 动词用法：有所–　　[词汇 U7.9]

根据提示回答问题

Answer the question based on the hint provided, as shown in the first item. In the second round, repeat each question aloud before answering it, and make sure you recognize the Chinese characters as well.

> **Note** the difference in meaning and usage:
>
> "有所" means "somewhat" or "to a moderate degree" (its colloquial counterparts are "有一些" or "有一点", which are used in an abstract sense). It must be followed by a disyllabic word, often an abstract *verb* which is also used as a *noun*, to form a four-character phrase. This form is normally used in semi-formal and formal styles. The following *nouns/verbs* are frequently used with the "有所–" phrase. However, do **not** use any disyllabic nouns/verbs freely as many may not fit the form or meaning.
>
> | 发展 | 改善 | 改进 | 增长 | 增加 | 上升/下降 |
> |------|------|------|------|------|-----------|
> | fāzhǎn | gǎishàn | gǎijìn | zēngzhǎng | zēngjiā | shàngshēng / xiàjiàng |

1. 以前这里环境污染很严重，最近几年情况怎么样？　(改善)　→　最近几年情况有所改善。

2. 以前这是最落后的城市之一，现在经济怎么样？　(发展)　→　现在经济有所发展。

3. 以前来这里工作的大学毕业生很少，现在人数怎么样？(增加)　→　现在人数有所增加。

4. 政府的新经济政策给这个地区带来什么变化？　(中小企业；发展)→　中小企业有所发展。

5. 最近几年这个城市的房地产情况怎么样？　(房价；上升)　→　房价有所上升。

第三课·城市发展与变化

U7-3.2-F 数据表达：率、倍、比例、大约、将近 [词汇 U7.10]
根据提示回答问题

This section works on **number and data expressions**. Answer the questions based on the hints provided. In the second round, repeat each question before answering it, and recognize the Chinese characters as well.

> 率: 增长率 就业率 离婚率 犯罪率
> lǜ zēngzhǎnglǜ jiùyèlǜ líhūnlǜ fànzuìlǜ

例：和去年相比，今年的经济发展情况怎么样？　　(+5%)

→ 今年的经济增长率是5%。

1. 这个城市大学毕业生就业情况怎么样？　　(过去三年，88%)

→ 过去三年里，大学毕业生的就业率是88%。

2. 近年来大城市的离婚率有什么变化？　　(以前=10%，**现在**= 30%，**上升**)

→ 以前离婚率是10%，现在上升到30%了。

3. 这里的流动人口很多，对社区的治安有什么影响？(犯罪率 +2%，使___ 上升)

→ 流动人口使犯罪率上升了2%。

> 倍 比例 大约 将近
> bèi bǐlì dàyuē jiāngjìn

Note: "大约" and "将近" can be abbreviated as "约" and "近". More notes on these words are provided under "**Forms and Structures**" in the Textbook.

Answer the following questions based on the information provided.

例：和20年前相比，现在的单身人数*增加了多少*？ (before: 5m; now: 10m)

→ 和20年前相比，现在的单身人数<u>比</u>20年前<u>增加了 一倍</u>。

现在的单身人数<u>是</u>20年前的<u>两倍</u>。

1. 今年的毕业人数有多少？是5年前的几倍？（150,000; 3 times as much）

→ 今年的毕业人数有15万，是五年前的3倍。

2. 这个学校的师生比例是多少？ （roughly 1:20）

→ 这个学校的师生比例大约是1比20。

3. 这个城市的人口里，男性的比例占多少？ （roughly 51%）

→ 这个城市的人口里，男性比例大约占51%。

4. 现在这个城市的人口有多少？（approaching 5 million）

→ 现在这个城市的人口将近500万。

U7-3.2-G 图表解说 [词汇 U7.10]

看图表选择适当的回答

This drill works on frequently used four-character stock expressions related to **data and graphs**. Look at the graph and choose the best phrase to answer the question. In the second round, repeat each question aloud and then answer in a complete sentence. You are expected to read the Chinese characters as well.

Before starting the drill, read vocabulary "词汇U7.10" aloud with comprehension.

逐渐增加	逐渐上升	迅速下降	迅速减少	上下波动
zhújiànzēngjiā	zhújiànshàngshēng	xùnsùxiàjiàng	xùnsùjiǎnshǎo	shàngxiàbōdòng
持续下滑	有所增长	保持稳定	稳定增长	增幅较大
chíxùxiàhuá	yǒusuǒzēngzhǎng	bǎochíwěndìng	wěndìngzēngzhǎng	zēngfújiàodà

1. 这些数据说明就业机会是什么情况？　　　　（逐渐增加　　迅速减少　　保持稳定）
2. 这些数据表明犯罪率有什么变化？　　　　　（逐渐上升　　逐渐下降　　上下波动）
3. 这些数据表明出生率呈什么趋势？　　　　　（逐渐上升　　逐渐下降　　上下波动）
4. 这些数据显示离婚率有什么趋势？　　　　　（迅速上升　　逐渐上升　　保持稳定）
5. 这些图表显示经济的发展怎么样？　　　　　（持续下滑　　有所增长　　稳定增长）
6. 这些数据显示的增长幅度(增幅)怎么样？　　（增幅很大　　增幅较大　　增幅较小）

U7-3.2-H 回答问题：谈谈自己熟悉的一个城市

Review the following sentence forms and expressions. Then answer the questions as if you were being interviewed by a Chinese school newsletter editor. Incorporate an expression from the list in the box in your answer.

有些数据表明	有数据显示	研究表明	据报道	据统计
yǒuxiē shùjù biǎomíng	yǒushùjù xiǎnshì	yánjiūbiǎomíng	jùbàodào	jùtǒngjì

1. 那个城市人口发展情况有什么变化？增长迅速还是缓慢？
2. 那个城市治安情况和以前比起来怎么样？比如说，犯罪率情况？
3. 那个城市在环境保护方面情况怎么样？有所改善，还是有很大改善？
4. 最近一年来，那个城市的经济发展怎么样？快速增长，保持稳定，还是有所下滑？
5. 近几个月来，物价情况怎么样？有所上升/下降，比较稳定，还是上下波动？
6. 各行业情况怎么样？比如说，房地产、金融业、汽车工业等？
7. 现在就业机会是什么情况？就业率上升了还是下降了？
8. 据你预测，今后几年在什么方面会迅速上升/增长？什么方面会上下波动或者逐渐下降？

流利强化 Fluency Enhancement

 U7-3.11 语块练习

Chunking Exercise: Listen to and repeat the phrases aloud. Then type them with 100% accuracy.

U7-3.11-A 成语及常用词组 [词汇 U7.7]

1. 很多现代建筑和高楼大厦， 商业区繁华热闹， 看上去比较先进发达
2. 商店里人来人往， 超市里的物品应有尽有， 给人的感觉是商业兴旺发达
3. 没有文化气息， 商业气息浓厚， 有很浓厚的商业气息
4. 交通四通八达， 商店里五光十色， 到处灯火辉煌， 很有民族特色
5. 交通常常堵塞， 到处垃圾成堆， 街道上车辆拥挤， 市容比较脏乱
6. 给人印象最深的是那里的建筑， 最吸引人的是这里的摩天大楼
7. 以小吃闻名， 以民族特色闻名， 以商业为主， 以旅游业为主
8. 是历史名城， 是历史最悠久的城市之一， 是文化气息最浓厚的城市之一
9. 这个城市由五个区组成， 这个社区由一个商业区和三个住宅区组成
10. 令人遗憾的是这里的人口密度太大， 美中不足的是这里商业不够发达

U7-3.11-B 图表数据表达 [词汇 U7.8-7.10]

1. 有研究显示， 有数据显示， 图表显示， 专家预测， 据有关统计， 据有关报道
2. 就业率有所上升， 失业率有所下降， 人口持续增长， 物价持续上升， 保持稳定
3. 经济稳定发展， 快速增长， 逐渐增长， 逐渐下滑， 情况有所改善
4. 呈上升趋势， 呈下滑趋势， 出现下滑的现象， 出现持续增长现象
5. 城市居民消费， 城市人均收入， 大学生就业机会， 农村人口比例
6. 增长得很快， 上升得很慢， 增加了很多， 减少了很多， 逐渐增加/减少
7. 增长了一倍， 增加了一倍， 增长了将近8%， 增加了大约三分之一， 增幅很大
8. 有很大差别， 有很大不同， 有一些差别/区别， 有一些相似之处， 很相似

Speed Reading/Review: Follow the steps below.

1. Listen to and then read the dialogue within <u>four</u> minutes, focusing on words and expressions.
2. Without looking at the text, recall the details in Chinese, and then answer the questions.
3. Read the dialogue again and learn the new words and useful expressions.

去哪个城市？

王：	嘿(hēi)，小李，在那儿想什么呢——<u>闷闷不乐</u>的？	

李：咳(hāi)，还能想什么——还不都是找工作的事？

王：怎么？还没有找到工作？别急，慢慢来。

李：咳，不是没找到，是决定不了该去哪儿！你看，现在有两个公司愿意<u>雇</u>我，一个是在北京，另一个是在<u>杭州</u>，两家的<u>待遇</u>都差不多。

王：哟(yō)，别人找工作都是在一个地区找，你怎么是从北找到南啊？

李：咳，你不知道，虽然我这几年住在北京，而且男朋友也是北京人，可我自己是在南方长大的，<u>一直</u>想回南方去，所以我就几个地方都试试吧。现在可好了，一北一南，我真<u>拿不定主意</u>了。你说我该选哪个？

王：要我说啊，当然是<u>留</u>在北京好。你不看看，谁不想到北京来！这里是全国的政治、经济和文化中心，<u>信息</u>最快，文化生活也丰富。你看，有那么多的博物馆和名胜古迹……

李：没错，北京的好处谁都知道，可<u>长期</u>在这里生活我可<u>受不了</u>。<u>首先</u>，这里天气这么<u>糟</u>，春天风沙那么大，吹得<u>天昏地暗</u>，夏天热得你<u>头昏脑胀</u>，冬天呢，又冷得你连门都不想出！我到现在都还没<u>适应</u>呢。

闷闷不乐 mènmènbúlè	unhappy, depressed
雇 gù	to hire
杭州 Hángzhōu	(capital of Zhejiang province)
待遇 dàiyù	job package (salary and benefits)
一直 yìzhí	always, all along
拿主意 názhǔyì	to make the decision
拿不定主意 nábúdìngzhǔyì	cannot make up one's mind
留 liú	to stay where one is
信息 xìnxī	information
长期 chángqī	long term
受不了 shòubùliǎo	unable to bear or withstand
首先 shǒuxiān	first of all
糟 zāo	bad, rotten; a mess
天昏地暗 tiānhūndìàn	dark all over
头昏脑胀 tóuhūnnǎozhàng	dizzy
适应 shìyìng	to adapt, adjust

第三课·城市发展与变化

王：那有什么大不了的？不就是天气嘛，时间长了就适应了。

李：不光是天气不适应，还有这里食品我也吃不惯！不是面条、饺子就是大饼、馒头，太单调了，哪里比得上我们南方的饭菜！

王：这也没有什么大不了的，现在餐馆这么多，你只要有钱，想吃什么就吃什么。

李：可还有这居住环境呢？你看看，这大都市到处是高楼大厦，不光是车多人多、噪音大、空气污染严重，而且每天上下班要花多少时间坐车等车？要是再碰上堵车，那两个钟头都回不到家！

王：这个问题嘛——大概别的城市也都有吧？

李：有是有，但总比北京好多了！还有，南方啊山清水秀，风景比起北方来可美多了，一年四季都是绿绿的，到处是鲜花；空气也清新得多。还有……

王：好了好了，反正你是南方人，自然觉得南方什么都好。那你就去杭州好了，这个选择也不错。人们不是说"上有天堂，下有苏杭"吗？只是，你男朋友怎么办？他会愿意放弃他现在的工作跟你去吗？

李：这不是个简单的问题。对了，假如你的女朋友要你放弃这里的工作跟她走，你会怎么办？

王：我现在的问题啊，倒不是我愿不愿意放弃工作，而是她愿不愿意要我跟她走！

不光 bùguāng	not only
吃不惯 chībúguàn	not comfortable eating
面条 miàntiáo	noodles
饺子 jiǎozi	dumplings
大饼 dàbǐng	pancake
馒头 mántou	steamed bun
比得上 bǐdeshàng	on par with
都市 dūshì	metropolis
噪音 zàoyīn	noise
碰上 pèngshang	to bump into, happen
堵车 dǔchē	traffic jam
反正 fǎnzhèng	anway, anyhow
选择 xuǎnzé	choice, option; to choose
天堂 tiāntáng	heaven
苏杭 sūháng	abbr. for Sūzhōu and Hángzhōu
放弃 fàngqì	to give up
假如 jiǎrú	if, suppose

回答问题

1) 小李为什么闷闷不乐？

2) 小王为什么建议她留在北京？北京有哪些好处？

3) 小李对北京哪些方面不满意？

4) 小李认为去杭州有什么好处？

5) 去杭州对小李会有什么问题？

6) "上有天堂，下有苏杭"是什么意思？

7) 你认为小李应该怎么办？

做比较：小李认为北京和杭州有什么不同?

1) 在天气方面，_____不如_____，比如说_____。

2) 从食品上看，_____不如_____的丰富，比如说_____。

3) 与杭州比起来，北京的居住环境_____，因为_____。

4) 与北京相比，杭州的风景_____，比如说，_____。

U7-3.13 流利练习：比较不同特点 (5分钟)

Fluency Drill: Listen to the following passage. After each sentence, pause for <u>two</u> to <u>three</u> seconds, and then repeat the whole sentence aloud from memory. You should repeat each sentence until you can say the sentence smoothly and accurately with the correct tones.

说到北方和南方的不同，人们首先想到的是气候上的差别。北方比较寒冷干燥，有的地区四季分明，有的地区冬季较长；而南方却比较温暖潮湿，冬季较短。另外，北方南方在地理特点上也不同：北方平原较多，一望无际，让人感觉特别开阔。山大，矿藏也很丰富。南方却是另一种景象：丘陵多、湖泊多，山清水秀，一年四季鲜花不断。

在饮食方面，北方和南方也有很大差别。比如说，北方以面食为主，馒头、包子、面条、大饼都是家常便饭，出产的蔬菜水果不如南方的多。而南方的主食为大米，做菜的方式也多种多样。相比之下，南方的食物比较丰富。

U7-3.14 写作练习：描述城市特色/印象 (10分钟)

Writing Exercise: Imagine a Chinese friend is seeking your help. He/she wants to study in your home country and experience life in a major city there. Respond to him/her with descriptions of two cities as well as your recommendation. Use general statements with supporting details, and incorporate appropriate four-character idioms, sentence patterns and key structures covered in this and previous lessons. Check your usage accuracy and the Chinese characters for any typing errors.

U7-3.15 词语自测：城市发展变化 (10分钟)

Vocabulary Self-Testing: Use the <u>timed memory test</u> method. Time yourself for <u>five</u> minutes to see how many items you can reproduce in the following categories. Type your items in pinyin or Chinese characters. Then check your glossary lists to see any words/phrases you may have missed.

1. Adjectives and descriptive phrases associated with a city (including our-character idioms and other stock expressions)
2. Words and expressions associated with data presentation and graph description
   - Words indicating positive conditions or results (*grow, stabilize...*)
   - Words indicating unstable or negative conditions or results (*fluctuate, fall...*)
   - Expressions associated with the source of information (e.g., *experts estimate, it was reported...*)
3. Additional words from listening/reading: Review the additional words and expressions in the listening/reading passages, e.g., "北方与南方", and "去哪个城市？". Look at the glossaries accompanying the texts and try to memorize 10-15 useful words or expressions. Then test yourself by typing them out in Chinese and English.

第 四 课   **介绍城市**
Lesson 4   INTRODUCING CITIES

U7-4.2 比较两个城市

This task reviews both core and advanced vocabulary while developing fluency in short paragraphs for semi-formal style. Each item focuses on a comparative structure or expression.

First read the example, and then answer the question using the key pattern/expression with details based on the hints provided. You must use appropriate connectives (比方说, 比如说, 而且, 但, 也, etc.) to provide linkage and transition. For best results, also type your answers out after your oral composition.

Pattern 1: 从……上看/在……方面, A和B有很多相似之处。比方说, ……

> **表面**   上海和纽约: 高楼大厦、摩天大楼, 繁华热闹, 商业发达, 拥挤……
>
> 从表面上看, 上海和纽约有很多相似之处。比方说, 两个城市都非常繁华热闹, 有很多高楼大厦和世界有名的摩天大楼, 商业很发达, 但街道比较窄、市中心让人感觉比较拥挤、吵闹。

练习: 上海和台北比起来怎么样?

> **交通**   上海和台北: 车多, 拥挤, 经常发生交通堵塞……

Pattern 2: 在……方面, A 和B(没)有很大/一些差别。比如说, ……

> **饮食**   北方和南方: 北方吃面食(包子、饺子、面条), 南方吃米饭, 菜多
>
> 在饮食方面, 北方和南方有很大差别。比如说, 北方人多半吃面食, 如包子、饺子、面条, 等等; 而南方人多半吃米饭, 菜的种类也比较丰富。

练习: 北京和上海比起来有什么不同?

> **城市特色**   北京和上海: 北京—名胜古迹、古代建筑、历史文化
>
>   上海—商业发达、现代建筑、繁华热闹

Pattern 3: 在……方面, A不如B / A不如B+褒义形容词

> **生活**   北京和上海: 上海食品丰富, 购物方便、便宜
>
> 在生活方面, 北京不如上海。比如说, 北京的食品不如上海的丰富, 购物也不如上海方便、便宜。

练习: 西部城市和东部城市比起来有哪些不同?

> **经济**   西部城市和东部城市: 东部经济、商业发达、发展迅速; 西部发展缓慢
>
> **水能资源**   东部城市和西部城市: 西部江河多, 用水能发电, 电力充足

Pattern 4: 相比之下，B (在⋯⋯方面) 比A更_____；_____多了

> 这个城市和那个城市：经济发展 _____ 比_____快
>
> 相比之下，这个城市<u>在经济发展方面</u>比那个城市更快。

练习: 广东和四川有什么不同?

　　广东和四川：就业机会 _____ 比_____多，广东靠近港口，工业、商业发达

Pattern 5: 与A相比/比起来，B(在⋯⋯方面)很/比较/非常_____；_____多了

> 大都市和小城市：不太拥挤；生活节奏慢一点
>
> <u>与大都市相比</u>，小城市不太拥挤，而且生活节奏没有大都市那么快。

练习: 西部城市与东部城市有什么主要区别?

　　西部城市和东部城市：山多、交通运输不够方便，商业贸易不够发达

单元测试与报告 Unit Assignments

For the unit review and assignments, please consult Appendices 1-3 for a guide on language use, grammar, and discourse structure.

U7-4.3 词语测试：本单元词语句式及语言结构

Vocabulary Test : Review the words and expressions in this unit and complete the vocabulary test assigned by your teacher.

U7-4.4 课堂报告：介绍城市概况；城市情况访谈

1. 介绍城市概况

City Profile Presentation: If you choose this project, prepare your slide presentation based on the following categories. Use the worksheet for your notes. You are NOT allowed to read from your scripts during your presentation. However, you may include keywords or some phrases (not sentences) in your slides as hints.

连接性词语:

虽然⋯⋯，但⋯⋯	一方面⋯⋯，(而)另一方面 ⋯⋯
除了⋯⋯以外, 还⋯⋯	另一个有意思的方面是⋯⋯
由于⋯⋯/因为⋯⋯, 所以⋯⋯	据报道/据统计/据专家预测
据XX说⋯⋯	有数据表明/显示, ⋯⋯
在(我, 他们)看来，⋯⋯	与⋯⋯比起来/相比
比如说，⋯⋯	不过
在⋯⋯方面, ⋯⋯	还有一点
从⋯⋯上看, ⋯⋯	总的来说

资 料 表
Worksheet

城市名称		
地理特点	位于, 靠近, 在X和Y之间, 离X不远, 由X、Y和Z组成	
气 候	四季分明, 四季如X, 寒冷, 炎热, 干燥, 多风/雨/雪, 潮湿, 气温最高/低……, 热得/冷得人……	
自然资源	以X为主/闻名, 丰富, 贫乏, 充足, 居第X位	
人口(数据)	大约, 将近, 占	
城市特色	被人们称为……, 以X闻名, 最吸引人的是, 最有特色的是	
主要经济	以X为主, 先进, 落后, 发展迅速/缓慢, 下滑	
就业数据	有所上升/下降, 稳定	
发展变化数据	发展很快/缓慢, 持续增长, 上下波动, 有所下降, 上升了X%, 倍, −率	
环 保	造成, 带来, 对X有利/有害, 有所改善, 采取措施	
其 他	在X方面很有特色, 很有名	

2. 模拟表演：城市情况访谈

Simulation: The Interview about a City: If you choose this project, read the following scenarios and preparation guidelines.

A角：你是中国一个地方电视台记者，要采访一个外国人，向他/她了解一个城市的情况。

B角：你是一个在中国工作或者学习的外国人。电视台记者向你了解你自己国家的一个城市的情况。你回答问题，并详细介绍情况。

Preparation: Read the following interview first. Then prepare notes about a city in your home country addressing these questions. You can also use the above worksheet and useful phrases, and add your own questions as well. However, you are not allowed to read from your notes or script during your interview, which means, you might need to memorize the questions and answers.

了解一个城市的情况

开头：您好，我叫(名字)，是(身份)。我想了解一下你们国家的城市发展情况。能不能请您给我介绍一下您熟悉的一个城市?

被访者回答：当然可以，我可以给您介绍一下(城市名)的情况。

提问：

1. 这个城市在什么地方? 靠近哪里?

2. 在地理环境和气候方面，这个城市有什么有利或者不利条件?

3. 这个城市大概有多少人口? 人口发展情况怎么样?

4. 你能不能给我描述一下这个城市的市容和外观 (看上去给人什么印象)?

5. 能不能请您谈一下这个城市的主要特色? (以……闻名、文化、建筑、名胜古迹等)

6. 与其他城市相比，这个城市最有特色、最吸引人的是什么?

7. 这个城市的经济有什么特点?

8. 近几年来，这里的就业情况怎么样?

9. 很多城市都有环保方面的问题，这个城市在这方面怎么样?

10. 最近几年来有什么特别的发展和变化?

11. (其他方面)

结束：听起来这个城市(发展不错, 很有意思, 等等)…… 好, 很高兴今天能听您介绍_____的情况，希望我今后有机会去那里看看。谢谢!

U7-4.5 语段写作：比较城市

Essay: Review the revised version of the sample paragraphs in Lesson 4. Write a comparative essay about two cities, following the tips in the lesson. Paragraph 1 outlines City A, and Paragraph 2 discusses some aspects of City B in comparison with City A. Remember, City A in the comparative paragraph is the reference city, not the topic.

活动程序和要求 Guidelines and Instructions for the Tasks

1. 阅读讨论活动要求 Guidelines for the Reading and Discussion Activities

Your good preparation for and active participation in the class discussions are required. Follow the instructions below (unless otherwise specified by your instructor).

For reading texts: You are expected to read the text in advance as you need to answer comprehension questions and share views in class. You can use a notebook or flashcards to collect useful words and expressions from the reading passages.

For your assigned task: If you have been assigned to lead a class discussion activity (by yourself or your group), you (or your group) should also prepare your activity by following these guidelines:

1) Keep your activity steps simple, clear, and efficient; do not try to accomplish too many things.
2) Limit your new vocabulary terms, if any, to <u>five</u>. Write the new terms on the blackboard to facilitate comprehension.
3) Have your outline, procedure, or script checked by your teacher in advance.

辩论活动说明 Instructions for the Debate

1) 中国城市化问题

辩论：会造成什么问题？有什么解决办法？

Work in three groups: Two groups of equal numbers are to conduct a debate on the issue of urbanization, and one group plays the role of the audience or judges. Your teacher will time your speech and monitor the turns (e.g., each speaker talks for a maximum of 60 seconds at a time). The audience or judges should take notes, vote for a winner, and explain the decision.

Preparation: Each group needs some pre-debate preparation to discuss strategies and speaking sequences. The audience group should also prepare a list of evaluation criteria.

2. 情景模拟任务准备 Preparing for the Simulation Tasks

任务1：介绍地区概况和公司发展计划 Presenting the Profile of an Area and Company's Development Plans

角色 Roles	公司代表(2人)，求职毕业生 (其他同学扮演) Company representative (2) , college graduates/job seekers (played by classmates)
情景/任务 Scenario/Task	你们是一个落后地区的发展公司的代表。在一个工作招聘会上，你们向求职的大学毕业生介绍地区概况和公司发展计划，希望吸引高校毕业生到自己公司工作；回答求职毕业生的问题。 You represent a company from an underdeveloped area. At a job fair, you try to attract college graduates (job seekers) to work for your company. Present the profile of the area and some attractive development plans and employment packages. Also interact with the job seekers by answering their questions.
要求 Presentation Requirements	时间长度：8–10分钟。可以用图片、图表，但不能用稿子或提示卡。 Time limit: 8-10 minutes for the simulation. You can use slides, pictures, charts, or brochures to enhance your presentation. However, you are not allowed to read from your script or any index cards.

任务2：电视访谈：城市化问题和解决措施 A TV Talk Show: Issues and Solutions

角色 Roles	节目主持人(1人)，市政府官员(1人)，市民代表(1人)，专家(1人)，观众(其他同学) Host (1), government official (1), city resident (1), urban development expert (1) , audience (classmates)
情景/任务 Scenario/Task	大量农村人口进入城市造成这个城市的很多问题，如就业、住房、治安、教育，等等。地方电视台于是推出一个访谈节目，请大家来讨论城市化造成的问题和解决办法。节目主持人简单介绍访谈话题，也介绍来宾(guests)。然后开始提问，请来宾表达自己的看法，提出解决办法。观众有机会提问。 The expanding urban population has created many problems in this city with regard to employment, housing, education, and public security. The local TV station is therefore presenting a talk show, inviting people to discuss the issues and seek solutions. The host (played by the teacher or a student) briefly introduces the discussion topic today as well as the invited guests (played by students). Then the host starts the discussion session by asking each guest to express their views. At the end of the show, the host also opens the floor for suggestions.
要求 Presentation Requirements	时间长度：15分钟。可以用图片、图表或数据提示卡，但不能用稿子或其他提示卡。 Time limit: 15 minutes for the simulation. You can use pictures or charts to illustrate your points, or a data info card or sheet to read some numbers. However, scripts, index cards or other aids are not allowed.

3. 调研报告任务说明 Instructions for the Research Project

Work in small groups or individually on one of the following topics for your project. First read all the project descriptions below, and then choose one topic to work on. Follow the requirements specified under each topic.

a. 高校毕业生就业率 College Graduates' Employment Rate

查阅你自己的国家或城市的高校毕业生就业率；查阅两年的资料，用适当的数据和图表报告调查结果，比较就业率的变化，说明原因和自己的看法。

b. 城市发展民意调查 Opinion Poll on Urban Development

设计一个调查问卷，调查同学和其他人对城市发展、人口膨胀的看法和解决措施。在班上报告调查结果，并谈自己的看法。

c. 自己国家城市情况 Cities in Your Country

了解你自己国家中两个城市近10年的情况(如，人口增长或离婚率、犯罪率、失业率等)。报告调查结果，并比较两个城市的不同。

d. 一个中国城市 A Chinese City

(See the sample paragraphs below for a general guide.)

了解并报告一个中国城市的发展概况。报告中需要包括城市的主要信息、文化特色，发展变化、数据、以及问题和措施。(请看以下写作样例)

语段示例：介绍中国城市上海
Sample Paragraphs: Introducing the Chinese City—Shanghai

This section provides some sample paragraphs. Read the example and note the topic sentences and supporting details.

例1：开头简介

Brief introduction to highlight the main features of the city

> 　　上海是一个先进发达、繁华热闹的现代化城市，也是世界上最大的城市之一。上海位于中国东部,紧靠东海。这里的气候四季分明，雨水和阳光都很充足。由于自然环境和资源条件很好，海边的地理位置对经济发展和贸易也很有利，所以上海的轻工业、商业、金融、外贸等一直都很发达，可以说多年来在经济和贸易上是中国的"龙头"。

例2：发展变化

Give examples to illustrate major developments, using numbers and ranking to emphasize importance. Add a picture or two to make deeper impressions.

> 　　近年来上海的发展变化很大，特别是上海浦东开发区，已经迅速成为上海最现代化的国际经济、金融、贸易的中心。这里新建了很多现代化的建筑和摩天大楼，如金茂大厦、东方明珠电视塔等，其中东方明珠电视塔高468米，是上海最高的建筑物，也是高度居亚洲第一位，世界第三位的电视塔。

例3：人口增长数据 (数据来源: 上海市第五次人口普查公报及上海概览网页)

Present supporting data. Use graphs or charts to facilitate understanding.

从1949年以来，上海的人口增长迅速。据报道，1949年上海人口为520万，1990年为1,334万，增长了约1.5倍。从1990年到2000年，人口增长到1,674万，10年间增长率为25%。如果从1949年算起，在这51年中人口增加了约1,154万，也就是说，2000年的人口是1949年的三倍多，其中城镇人口占76.4%，农村人口23.6%。但据统计，近几年来，上海市区人口的出生率有所下降。

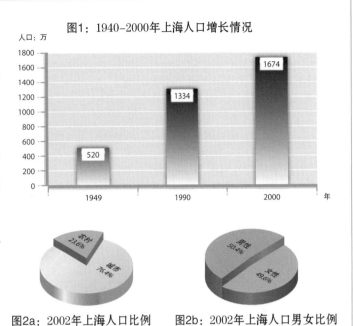

图1：1940-2000年上海人口增长情况

图2a：2002年上海人口比例　图2b：2002年上海人口男女比例

例4：城市的新发展：问题和解决办法

Discuss an issue and possible solutions. Use supporting data if any and give a concrete example with relevant details. Add an image to illustrate and enhance the presentation.

由于上海人口多，环境保护是一个很重要的问题。1991年上海政府用于环保的投资不到8亿元，而2006年的环保投资近311亿元，15年内增加了近40倍。环保项目之一是市区公共绿地的建设。

为了改善居住环境和空气，市政府采取了很多绿化城市的措施，在市区内建造了一些公园和公共绿地，如位于杨浦区的黄兴公园就是上海市内最大的公共绿地。这些措施不但对居住环境有利，而且也给居民提供了很多娱乐休闲的地方。